KEKĀVALI

Poet Moropanta's

KEKĀVALI

A Series of the Peacock's Screams

Translated by
P.V. BOBDE

With a foreword by
Dr. G.M. RANADE

MOTILAL BANARSIDASS PUBLISHERS
PRIVATE LIMITED • DELHI

First Edition: Delhi, 1994

ISBN: 81-208-1115-1

Also available at:

MOTILAL BANARSIDASS

41 U.A. Bungalow Road, Jawahar Nagar, Delhi 110 007
120 Royapettah High Road, Mylapore, Madras 600 004
16 St. Mark's Road, Bangalore 560 001
Ashok Rajpath, Patna 800 004
Chowk, Varanasi 221 001

PRINTED IN INDIA
BY JAINENDRA PRAKASH JAIN AT SHRI JAINENDRA PRESS,
A-45 NARAINA, PHASE I, NEW DELHI 110 028
AND PUBLISHED BY NARENDRA PRAKASH JAIN FOR MOTILAL
BANARSIDASS PUBLISHERS PVT. LTD., BUNGALOW ROAD,
DELHI 110 007

To
Madhukar
My younger brother
Whose participation in India's
Freedom Movement and deep
study of Vedānta have earned
a place of pride in my heart

FOREWORD

To put the thoughts and feelings expressed in one language into another is generally known as translation. But it would be ludicrous to say that merely the use of a word for word in other language is translation in the true sense of the term. For one who ventures to take up the task of translation it is absolutely necessary to possess the capacity to enter into the heart and mind of the author, whose work is to be translated and also to identify himself completely with the feelings and sentiments of the author. Without close acquaintance with the language from which a work is to be translated, as also a good command over the language into which the translation is to be taken up, one need not pose to brave this danger involved in the translation work. As a matter of fact, to render from poetry into prose in one and the same language is in itself not an easy job. It should not therefore be difficult to imagine how it would be an uphill task to translate even into prose a work of poetry in any other language. Poetry is the supermost form of expression, rarely possessed by one amongst thousands. At times, powerful feelings and sentiments stored up in the heart of a poet, do suddenly burst in the form of words, and this spontaneous overflow assumes the shape of a gifted piece of poetry. This is in fact only a God's gift not available to all. Now to transmit the sentiments of such a gifted poet into the hearts of readers is not an easy job without a thorough knowledge of words and idioms of language. In addition, it is also essential to be in possession of the capacity to identify one's self completely with the poet's inner self, his heart and mind.

Moropanta is supposed to be a jewel in the crown of Marathi classical poetry. He possessed wonderful mastery over Marathi and Sanskrit. He had exclusive capacity to wield words into marvellous structure. He gave vent to his thoughts, feelings and sentiments in eloquent language. Rhyming was a child's play to him. Right from a simple one-letter rhyme, he could with remarkable ease rhyme two whole lines or *caraṇs* of a stanza with different meanings to the great astonishment of the readers and has naturally evoked their high admiration. Moropanta's poetry is bedecked with Sanskrit, erudition, jugglery of word-structure, fine arguments and skilful advocacy of his own cause rendering numerous illustrations from the *Purāṇas.*

A mere literal translation of this type of scholarly poetry is not enough. Unless the whole poetic beauty in its original form is brought to the experience of the reader, the translation might be of no avail. Śrī Bobde wields a remarkable mastery both on Marathi and English languages. By God's grace, a sympathetic and sentimental mood, so necessary for appreciating poetry, has been bestowed upon him. This is why he could, during the preceding years, successfully render one hundred eight *Abhaṅgas* of Saint Jñāneśvara into lucid English. He has thus obliged the English knowing readers by enabling them to approach as near as possible the mystic and spiritual wealth of the Marathi saint-poets. Śrī Bobde has given a beautiful English prose rendering of the one hundred and twenty one ślokas of *Kekāvali* which would certainly enable the readers to have a live experience of the poet's feelings with all the finest points. The *Kekāvali* is a reflection of Moropanta's mental torture, his restlessness for salvation, his unbearable impatience for communion with God, his pitiful entreaties to deliver him of all sins as also the intelligent arguments put forth to establish and justify his stand. To transplant the poet's inner self into the reader's heart and mind is in itself a great achievement of Śrī Bobde.

Moropanta is primarily a very sensitive and sentimental poet having full faith in God. The *Kekāvali* is an outburst of his restlessness and passionate longing for God coming about when he began to notice the signs of his approaching end. Śrī Bobde, it seems, has been successful in having an access to Moropanta's heart and to drink deep all his restlessness, or else, how could he render the same into an accurate and vivid English prose? The reader does not find the slightest difficulty in understanding the mythological episodes and the various characters involved in them. The Glossary given at the end of the book as also the footnotes will go a long way in facilitating the reader to know the meanings of certain difficult words and be introduced with unfamiliar mythological references.

It is a universal experience that in old age, as one approaches the ultimate destination of life—death—one longs to look back upon one's own life in a very dispassionate and detached manner, with a view to enumerating the plus and minus points, achievements and failures, and yearns for a peaceful and contented departure from the world. This experience is universal in the sense that it is common to all irrespective of caste, creed or religion. The reader would not find it difficult to absorb the feelings of the poet for which he should be grateful to Śrī Bobde for providing him the opportunity to peep into the mind of the poet, who appears to voice the sentiments of all those, who are gradually heading towards the ultimate point of life, the irresistible death.

Prof. P.N. Joshi of Poona, in his Foreword to Śrī Bobde's book *Garland of Divine Flowers* has expressed a desire that 'Śrī Bobde, who possesses a sentimental mind may get an opportunity to add to this wreath numerous other flowers'. Prof. Joshi should be happy to note that Śrī Bobde has come up to the mark by presenting this beautiful English prose rendering of Moropanta's *Śloka Kekāvali*. This would also, no doubt, give contentment of an achievement to Śrī Bobde and pleasure to his friends.

Jabalpur (M.P.) G.M. Ranade

CONTENTS

PREFACE

A thing of beauty is a joy for ever!
—Keats

I have great pleasure in presenting to the readers the English prose translation of *Kekāvali* the immortal poem of the great Marathi poet Moropanta of the eighteenth century. The poem is a precious gem in the treasure house of the Marathi poetry.

It is so exquisite that even after a long period of two hundred years, it has not lost its spell on the Marathi-speaking people even today and would doubtless continue to lure them for several generations to come! Instead of my describing the greatness of the poem to the readers, I would rather let them go through the poem and experience for themselves the grandeur and beauty of it. A reading of the poem is bound to remind the reader of Gurudeva Tagore's *Gitāñjali*.

Though the outward form and the way of exposition of these two poems differ, yet there is a point common in between them and that is the dialogue of the authors with the Supreme Lord and their quest for Him! Whereas Rabindranatha's poetry takes us to the Himalayan height of the Upaniṣadic thoughts, the poetry of Moropanta leads us to the sacred land of the doctrine of devotion as expounded in *Śrīmadbhāgavata*! *Kekāvali* could therefore be aptly called as the *Gītāñjali* of the eighteenth century!

While translating the poem, I have taken meticulous care to see that the translation reflects the original in its entirety. There are a number of mythological references appearing in the poem. With a view that the readers may be able to appreciate and enjoy the beauty of the poem without any difficulty I have given copious footnotes at the end of each stanza for their guidance. A glossary of important Sanskrit and Marathi words with their English equivalents is also appended to the book.

A short account of the life and literature of the poet is included in the book for information of the readers.

I am grateful to Dr. G.M. Ranade, a renowned scholar and a reputed Marathi writer, for going through the manuscript and writing Foreword to the book.

In order that the readers not acquainted with Marathi may appreciate the form and the beauty of the poem, I have reproduced the text of the entire poem in Roman script for their convenience. A chart showing the diacritical marks used in this book is appended for ready reference of the readers.

I have given captions to all the stanzas though these do not appear in the original.

I am grateful to Prof. G.W. Kaveeshwar of Indore, an eminent Indian philosopher and a renowned scholar, for having critically examined the manuscript of *Kekāvali* on my special request. A number of valuable suggestions made by him have been incorporated in the manuscript.

I have no doubt that the book would prove to be a source of joy to the readers.

Flat No. 72, Pocket F-25
Sector VII, Rohini,
Delhi-110085

P.V. BOBDE

POET MOROPANTA

His Life and Literature

Life

The famous Marathi poet Moropanta Parāḍakara was born in a poor Brahmin family at Panhālagaḍa (near Kolhapur) in 1729. His father Rāmājīpanta Parāḍakara was a devotee of Lord Gaṇeśa and so he 'christened' his second son as *Mayūra* (who later on became a reputed poet. *Mayūra* means a peacock. In vernacular it means *Mora*. Hence the poet's name—Mayūrapanta or Moropanta as *Mayūra* is regarded as a partial incarnation of Lord Gaṇeśa.

When Moropanta was of eleven, Rāmājīpanta left Panhālgaḍa where he was serving in the Kolhapur State regime and went to Baramati. There he secured a job under Bābuji Nāik Joshi, an influential nobleman of the region. Rāmājipanta, however, kept Moropanta at Panhālagaḍa with Pādhye Brothers for studies. These Pādhye Brothers were reputed Sanskrit scholars and were known for their wide learning. After having studied for a period of about twelve years, Moropanta left Panhālagaḍa to join his father at Baramati in 1753, where he lived till his death.

While at Panhālagaḍa, Moropanta, besides going through the various *Purāṇas*, epics like *Rāmāyaṇa* and *Mahābhārata* had also studied the works of Kālidāsa, Bhavabhūti and other Sanskrit poets. In addition, he studied carefully the works of the prominent Marathi poet-saints like Jñāneśvara, Ekanātha, Tukārāma and Rāmadāsa. He also acquainted himself with the poetry of other reputed saints like Tulsīdāsa, Kabīra and Narsī Mehatā.

Moropanta had an aptitude for composing poems and started his career as a poet by selecting mythological episodes for his poems. He soon attained the reputation of a distinguished poet. Impressed with his poetic genius, Bābuji Nāik Joshi of Baramati, a prominent nobleman, offered to become his patron and Moropanta accepted his patronage. After the death of Bābuji

Nāik, his son Pāṇḍuranga Nāik continued his patronage to Moropanta.

When Moropanta was sixty, he undertook the pilgrimage of Kāśī in the year 1790. His stay at Kāśī was for four months. The pundits there showered on him honours for his scholarship and his achievement in the field of poetry especially for his famous poetic work, the *Āryā Bhārata*. On his way back to Baramati, Moropanta went to Maheśvara to pay his respects to the saintly (widowed) reigning queen Ahilyābāī Holkar of immortal fame both for righteousness and administration. She was much pleased with his visit, gave him all honours due to a great poet and prevailed on him to stay at Maheśvara and spend the rest of his life under her patronage. Moropanta, however, did not agree. He had not forgotten the obligations of his patrons, the Nāiks and so declined the offer very courteously. Taking leave of Ahilyābāī, he made his way to Baramati. After his return, Moropanta composed the following couplet in honour of Ahilyābāī.

Devi Ahilyābāī jhālīsa jagatrayāta tū dhanyā
nanyāyadharma — niratā anyā kalimāji aikilī kanyā!

'Devi (Goddess in human form) Ahilyābāī, you are truly blessed in all the three worlds; in this (evil) Kaliyuga, I have heard of no other lady as steeped in Justice (in administration) and Righteousness (in personal life) as yourself!

Moropanta was of an amiable disposition. He was pure and kind at heart and was loved by all. He was an ardent devotee of Śrī Rāma and was all the while yearning for salvation. The end was slowly approaching. Finally, after having implored Lord Rāma earnestly for His kind Grace through his immortal outpourings — *Kekāvali*, he breathed his last in 1794, at the age of sixty-five!

Literature

सुश्लोक वामनाचा अभंगवाणी प्रसिद्ध तुकयाची ।
ओवी ज्ञानेशाची, तैसी आर्या मयूरपंताची । ।
(Suśloka Vāmanācā, abhaṅga vāṇī prasiddha Tukayācī,
Ovī Jñāneśācī, taisī āryā Mayūrpantācī.)

(Poet Vāmana[1] is famous for his *Śloka*, Tukārāma for his *Abhaṅga*[2], Jñāneśvara for his *Ovī* and Moropanta for his *Āryā*.)

Moropanta's contribution to Marathi poetry is great both in volume and depth. His total compositions (stanzas) exceed sixty thousand. Of these over forty thousand are *Āryās* (composed in Āryā metre). The rest are in other metres. The details of his works and the corresponding number of *Āryās* in which they are composed, are indicated below:

Mahābhārata	17,170
Rāmāyaṇa	16,000
Harivaṁśa	5,444
Kṛṣṇa Vijaya or *Bṛhaddaśama*	3,669
Mantra Bhāgavata	3,592
Brahmottara Khaṇḍa	1,200
	47,075
Other compositions (about)	10,000
	57,075
Roughly	60,000

Moropanta started his career as a poet by selecting for his subjects mythological themes. His first selections were from *Viṣṇu Purāṇa*, *Mārakaṇḍeya Purāṇa*, *Jaimini Aśvamedha* and *Brahmottara Khaṇḍa* on which he composed poems in Āryā metre.

1. Vāmana—A distinguished Marathi poet of the eighteenth century who preceded Moropanta. Vāmana was a great Sanskrit scholar and is popularly known as Vāmana Pandita. He enriched Marathi poetry by his Ślokas which are very popular because of their excellence in diction.
Tukayā: Is the prakṛta form of Tukārāma, the renowned poet-saint of Maharashtra. Famous for his Marathi *Abhaṅgas* (devotional poems).
Jñāneśvara: The illustrious poet-saint of Maharashtra. His great poetic works —*Jñāneśvarī* and *Amṛtānubhava* in Marathi are composed in *Ovī* metre.
2. It may be pointed out that the *Abhaṅga* and *Ovī* metres are peculiar to Marathi poetry.

Realising that his poetic pieces based on *Purāṇas* had gained immence popularity, he took up the *Mahābhārata* and the *Rāmāyaṇa* as subjects for his poems. These were followed by *Kṛṣṇa Vijaya* and *Mantra Bhāgavata*. He incorporated or rather intertwined the mantra "नमो भगवते वासुदेवाय" in his *Bhāgavata* and hence it is called *Mantra Bhāgavata*. Moropanta was a great Sanskrit scholar. Besides his main works on *Mahābhārata* and *Rāmāyaṇa* in Marathi, he wrote *Mantra Rāmāyaṇa* in Sanskrit which comprises of 4000 verses!

Moropanta also composed a number of poems on the life and teachings of the famous saints like Jñāneśvara, Nāmadeva, kabīra, Narsi Mehatā, Ekanātha, Rāmadāsa, Tukārāma and Tulasīdāsa. Moropanta's poetry can be classified into two parts—impersonal and personal. A very extensive part deals with the epics like *Rāmāyaṇa* and *Mahābhārata*. The other one though practically negligible in size, yet of not less importance relates to his individual self—the awareness of his inner frailties, the grip of worldly passions, the pricks of conscience that he had still to come out of the woods of sin, and a craving for deliverance from all these weaknesses, which are the hindrances in the way of the life's highest and noblest objective. The first part it appears was intended to impress the readers with his scholarship in Sanskrit by extensive employment of Sanskrit words in his poetry, the exuberant use of rhymes to exhibit his grip on language and the selections from a wide range of Sanskrit literature to display his erudition. In short, it was primarily the scholar Moropanta, who is seen reigning supreme over his domain of poetry till the year 1783, that is when he was fifty-four. The works composed in the subsequent period of his life however show a marked tilt to the spiritual and devotional outlook as evident from the subjects of his poetry such as praise of saints and Gods, sacred places, glory of God's name, entreaties to the Almighty for blessings etc. In this class of poetry, *Kekāvali* is the brightest star. In this poem he makes a stirring appeal from the innermost depths of his heart to God for bestowal of His Grace on him.

Kekāvali[1]: Of all the voluminous poetic works of Moropanta, the poem for which he is still remembered and will be remembered in future is his immortal *Śloka Kekāvali* composed in Pṛthvī Vṛtta. In this poem Moropanta refers to the saga of the great deeds of Lord Nārāyaṇa through His various incarnations. He is seen addressing to God in His different capacities—some times as the caretaker of the universe, sometimes as a generous donor, sometimes as the true enjoyer of the pleasures of life, sometimes as the protector of his devotees, sometimes as the father of the creation, sometimes as the destroyer of the wicked, sometimes as the sea of mercy and supports his case for his early uplift by citing a number of parallels from mythological anecdotes. While doing so, he has at times made very ingeneous arguments and exhibited the skill of a proficient pleader! The poet's inimitable diction in *Kekāvali*, the soaring flights of his fancy, the novelty and the nobleness of the theme, his dexterity in rhymings and his heart-felt yearning for God's early bestowal of His favour have all gone to make *Kekāvali* a great poem. One is tempted to read, re-read and recite the verses from it even today! The poem has retained its spell on the minds of the Marathi people even after a long span of two hundred years!

Moropanta's contribution to the Marathi poetry is immense and of a high order. A major portion of his poems is composed in Āryā Vṛtta metre of which he is regarded as the greatest exponent. Marathi poets did not know of this metre before Moropanta. It was he who introduced it in Marathi poetry and that too with such outstanding success.

Moropanta has used in his poems rhymes[2] so lavishly and

---

1. There is another poem of the poet bearing the same name, viz., Kekāvali. It is composed in Āryā Vṛtta metre and hence known as Aryā Kekavali. It is, however, not so famous.
2. It may be noted that poet has indulged at times in the exercise of too much of rhyming which has been criticised by some writers. However, the overall spark-ling beauty of the composition, coupled with the transparent sincerity of the personal conversational style vis-a-vis God Viṣṇu (Nārāyaṇa) should induce the reader to overlook that one alleged point of criticism; specially when the poet himself, with all humility disclaims perfection in his poem. (Vide verses 33, 37, 61)!

with so much skill that it is almost difficult to find a comparison to their use either in Sanskrit or in Marathi poetry. The ease with which he has used the rhymes in his poetry in Āryā Vṛtta is equally noticed in his poems composed in other metres as well, viz: Ovī, Dohā, Sākī, Pṛthvī, Śardulavikriḍita, etc.

To sum up, Moropanta has left an indelible mark on the Marathi poetry. The credit of making the Marathi language 'cultured', firstly by the introduction of Sanskrit words in poems in a large measure and secondly by replacement of the deformed and corrupt words prevalent in Marathi language by their refined or chaste forms goes to Moropanta. Further, it would be no exaggeration to say that Marathi poetry, what it is today owes a lot to him. His poetry has so far defied the ravages of time and shall doubtless continue to be ever fresh and be a source of joy to the generations to come.

SCHEME OF TRANSLITERATION

अ	a	ड्	ḍ
आ	ā	ढ्	ḍh
इ	i	ण्	ṇ
ई	ī	त्	t
उ	u	थ्	th
ऊ	ū	द्	d
ऋ	ṛ	ध्	dh
ॠ	ṝ	न्	n
ए	e	प्	p
ऐ	ai	फ्	ph
ओ	o	ब्	b
औ	au	भ्	bh
अं(ं)	ṁ	म्	m
अः (ः)	ḥ	य्	y
क्	k	र्	r
ख्	kh	ल्	l
ग्	g	व्	v
घ्	gh	श्	ś
ङ्	ṅ	ष्	ṣ
च्	c	स्	s
छ्	ch	ह्	h
ज्	j	ळ्	ḷ
झ्	jh	क्ष्	kṣ
ञ्	ñ	ज्ञ्	jñ
ट्	ṭ	त्र	tr
ठ्	ṭh		

[Nasal म् followed by श्, ष् or स् = ṁ]

के का व लि

KEKĀVALI

सदाश्रितपदा ! सदाशिवमनोविनोदास्पदा !
स्वदासवशमानसा ! कलिमलांतका ! कामदा !
वदान्यजनसद्गुरो ! प्रशमितामितासन्मदा
गदारिदरनंदकांबुजधारा ! नमस्ते सदा

Sadāśritapadā Sadāśivamanovinodāspadā !
Svadāsavaśamānasā ! Kalimalāntakā Kāmadā
Vadānyajanasadguro ! Praśamitāmitāsanmadā !
Gadāridaranandakāmbujadharā ! Naamaste Sadā !

1. I adore Thee at all times

To the Paramātman in the form of Lord Nārāyaṇa,[1]
At whose feet saints and devotees take refuge,
God Śaṅkara feels at ease,
Whose mind stands subjugated to his devotees,
Who wipes out sin from the minds of the villainous
Who fulfils the desires of the people
Who is the highest preceptor of the magnanimous souls,
Who has subdued the arrogance of innumerable wicked persons,
Who wields mace, wheel, conchshell, Nandaka sword and lotus,
I offer my salutations for ever and ever!

Sadāśritapadā! Sadāśivamanovinodāspadā!
Svadāsavaśamānasā! Kalimalāntakā! Kāmadā!
Vadānyajanasadguro! Praśamitāmitāsanmadā!
Gadāridaranandakāmbujadharā! Namaste sadā.

1. Although the poet was a prime devotee of Śrī Rāma, he had equal reverence for the other deities too. He firmly believed that all the deities are incarnations of the Supreme Spirit and that God Nārāyaṇa is also its Saguṇa form. In this verse there is no mention of any deity, but from the names of the weapons indicated, it can be safely surmised that it is Nārāyaṇa who is alluded to by the poet.

2. Even the great sinners were liberated by Thee!

O Lord, a particle of dust of Thy lotus feet is verily the source of the sin-purifying power of all the sacred things in the world. O Rādhāramaṇa, Thou hast been the saviour of even the devils who were verily the mountains of sin! The immoral Ajāmiḷa,[1] the cruel demon Agha,[2] Wily Pūtanā,[3] disguised as Gopī and a harlot like Piṅgalā[4] have all been liberated!! When grass comes into contact with fire, it is bound to be burnt to ashes!

Padābjaraja je tujhe sakalapāvanādhāra te;
Aghācalahi tārile bahu tuvāci Rādhārate;
Ajāmila, Aghāsura, Vrajavadhū Bakī, Pingalā,
Aśā gati dilī; ure na tṛṇa bheṭatā iṅgalā.

1. Ajāmiḷa was a Brahmin but was depraved. He had named one of his sons as 'Nārāyaṇa' and while breathing his last was all the while pining for him and incessantly uttering his name which resulted in his liberation! (*Bhāgavata Purāṇa*, Part VI, cantos 1, 2)
2. Agha the demon attempted to kill Lord Kṛṣṇa but was himself killed by the Lord and attained liberation! (A legend from *Bhāgavata Purāṇa*, X canto 12)
3. Bakī (or Pūtanā) was a female demon who tried to kill Kṛṣṇa. She was however killed by the Lord who bestowed on her liberation. In the third line of the stanza the names of the sinners who were liberated by God are mentioned. These are Ajāmiḷa, Aghāsura, Vrajavadhū, Bakī and Piṅgalā. All the commentators of *Kekāvali* have equated Vrajavadhū with the rest of the sinners named in the stanza. I, however, beg to differ from them. In my view the Vrajavadhū who were innocent and deeply devoted to Kṛṣṇa cannot, by any stretch of imagination, be termed as sinners and equated with the rest. I have therefore corelated the words Vrajavadhū and Bakī to mean Bakī in the disguise of Vrajavadhū.
4. Piṅgalā was a harlot but was emancipated due to her extreme devotion for God. (Ibid., XI canto 8)

3. The dust of Thy feet purifies sinners!

O Lord, it is not at all untrue as has been vouched by the wise men of righteous conduct, that numerous persons who were the very oceans of sins have been purified by the particles of dust of Thy feet. Moreover, the number of those who have been saying so is not limited to one or two but is by hundreds. Therefore, it would only prove my meanness if I alone were to declare such persons as unbelievable or untrustworthy.

Tujhyā bahuta śodhile aghanidhī padācyā raje;
Na te anṛta varṇitī budha janī sadācāra je;
Ase satata bolate śata, na eka te; mīca te
Pramāṇa na mhaṇo jarī, ucita mājhiyā nīcate.

4. Boundless is Thy grace!

Why then, O Lord, have I remained neglected so far? Am I not sinful? Or (if I am) has the stock of Thy grace been totally exhausted in the course of uplifting of the sinners? But this can never happen since Thou being the caretaker of this entire universe, the fund of Thy grace can have no end. Can it be that I might have escaped Thy notice? But this inference also is not tenable as the sun himself being Thy eye,[1] there is nothing that can remain hidden from Thee. Should I presume that I have incurred Thy displeasure because of my numerous failings? But then this presumption too does not appear to be appropriate for howsoever enraged a cow may be, her udder would yield only milk and not poison!

Tasāci uralo kasā? patita mī nase kāya? kī
Kṛpāci saralī? asehi na ghade jagannāyakī.
Nasena disalo kasā? nayana sarvasākṣī ravī
Viṣāda dharilā mhaṇo? na surabhī viṣa kṣira vī.

1. Refer *candramā manaso jātaḥ cakṣus sūryo ajāyata (Vedic Puruṣasūkta).* 'For the embodied Supreme Spirit the Moon became the mind, while Sun became the eye.'

5. O Govardhana-lifter why canst Thou not lift me?

O Lord, for protecting Gokula, Thou hadst lifted the Govardhana hill itself on the tip of Thy finger's nail.[1] On the famous occasion of 'Samudramanthana' Thou hadst also held with ease the mountain Mandara on Thy back.[2] Assuming the incarnation of Varāha, Thou hadst even taken out the earth (from Pātāla) with Thy tusks.[3] How then could I be so heavy with the load of sin that even Thou, the performer of these miraculous feats shouldst find it difficult to liberate me? O Lord, why dost Thou not save me?

Vrajāvana karāvayā vasavile nakhāgrī dharā,
Salīla tai mandarākhyahi naga svapṛṣṭhī dharā,
Varāhatanu gheunī ucalilī radagre dharā,
Sudurdhara tumhā kasā patita hā? na kā uddharā?

---

1. Once the cowherds in Vṛndāvana worshipped the Govardhana hill instead of God Indra. This enraged Indra and with a view to punish them he caused a heavy downpour to lash the hill. Lord Kṛṣṇa thereupon lifted the hill itself on the tip of his finger like an umbrella and protected the entire Gokula under it! (*Bhāgavata Purāṇa*, X-canto 24)
2. With a view to secure the nectar, both the gods and the demons began churning the sea with the Mandara mountain as the churner. But soon the mountain started slowly going down. God Nārāyaṇa thereupon, assuming the form of a tortoise held it firmly on his back and prevented it from going down. This is the second of the ten incarnations of Lord Nārāyaṇa. (Ibid, XI-canto 4).
3. When the earth started sinking into Pātāla, Lord Nārāyaṇa assumed the form of a boar and took it out of the sea by his tusks and held it over the surface of water. This is the third incarnation of Lord Nārāyaṇa. (Refer *Harivaṁsha Purāṇa, Bhaviṣya Parva*, cantos 34, 35 Gita Press edition.)

6. O the protector of the devotees, fulfil thy vow!

O Lord, Thy vow is to protect Thy humble devotees. Thou art like a wild fire destroying the forest of the worldly calamities. Thou art the only one who art the foremost to run to the rescue of Thy devotees in times of their distress who have come to take refuge at Thy feet. Please tell me who it was that exhibited glaring compassion for the elephant named Gajendra in his hour of peril,[1] for Draupadī in the moments of her distress[2] and for Arjuna in leading him to success in the great Bhārata War,[3] if not Thou?

Natāvana dhṛtavratā! jvalana tūci bādhāvanī,
Padapraṇatasaṅkaṭī prajava tūci, bā dhāvanī,
Dayā prakaṭa dākhavī kavaṇa, sāṅga, tyā vāraṇī,
Satīvyasanavāraṇī, jayajayārtha tyā vā raṇī?

1. The legend 'Gajendra Mokṣa' runs thus—Gajendra is the name of the elephant. Once when he came to a lake for sporting, a crocodile caught his leg and attempted to kill him. He, therefore, earnestly implored lord Viṣṇu for help who taking pity on him, immediately appeared on the scene, and ripping the jaws of the crocodile with His divine wheel 'Sudarśana', set Gajendra free and released both of them from the curse to which they were subject. (*Bhāgavata Purāṇa* VIII, cantos 2, 3, 4)
2. The poet here alludes to the trying episodes in the life of Draupadī, wife of the Pāṇḍavas, e.g., dishonour to which she was subjected in the court of the Kauravas, alms sought by the irrascible sage Durvāsa with a view to test her hospitality and how Lord Kṛṣṇa by His yogic powers, ran down to her help and rescued her from the predicaments. (*Mahābhārata*, Sabhā Parva, cantos 67, 68 and Vana Parva, canto 263)
3. It is well-known how Lord Kṛṣṇa acting as Arjuna's charioteer in the Bhārata War, led him to victory by resorting to numerous devices.

7. Thou condescendest to assist the low!

O the Supreme Lord, even Thy consort Lakṣmī was not considered by Thee fit enough to enjoy an equal status in the amorous game of love-making, but Thou willingly condescended to serve Thy subordinate (Arjuna) as his horse-attendant! Thy hands which wouldst not have taken pains except for drawing 'Patrāvalī' on the breast of Thy beloved consort[1] undertook a mean and laborious work of picking up the 'Patrāvalī' on the occasion of the Rājasuya Yajña performed by the Pāṇḍava King Dharmarāja!![2]

Supātra na Ramāhi yadratisukhāsa dārā parī,
Asā prabhuhi sevakā bhajasi khāsadārāparī,
Priyākucatatī jihī na bahuvāra patrāvaḷī
Tihī amita kāḍhilya nṛpamakhāta patrāvaḷī.

---

1. In olden days, it was customary for the ladies to get 'Patrāvalī' (attractive and colourful designs of creepers and plants) drawn with pounded sandalwood on their hands, cheeks and breasts. Many a time such designs were drawn by their husbands themselves. Several Sanskrit Poets refer to this romantic practice. Thus Kalidāsa in *Raghuvaṁsha*, III -55, IV-72, *Ṛtusaṁhāra*, IV -5, 13 VI -7 etc.
2. In the 'Rājasūya Yajña' (a great sacrifice performed by a paramount monarch), Lord Kṛṣṇa took upon himself willingly as an act of moral merit the duty of removing the 'Patrāvali' (plates made of leaves tacked together) on which the invitees had dined!

8. A host desires that all his guests return satisfied

O Lord, Thou hast not conferred Thy favours on me till now and so I call Thee idle. But now I feel that my charge of idleness against Thee like the charge of theft[1] against Thee by Sūrya's friend Satrājita, is false and unfair to Thee. When a generous host after having invited to dinner innumerable persons and satisfied them fully comes to know that through oversight someone has remained without food, he immediately serves food to him also. However, he (host) does feel the pricks of conscience for the inadvertent act of omission committed by him!

Na pāvasi mhaṇoni mī mhaṇatase tulā āḷaśī;
Barī na asadukti, he, Ravisakhotthitā āḷaśī;
Asaṅkhya jana tarpile, kṣudhita ekalā jemanī
Cukela, tari tyāsa de, pari vadānya lāje manī.

1. The episode about the theft of the 'Syamantaka' gem as narrated in *Bhāgavata* is as under: Satrājita was Sūrya's friend. Sūrya had given him a unique gem called Syamantaka which was lost. A false accusation of theft was levelled by Satrājita against Śrī Kṛṣṇa. After great efforts, Śrī Kṛṣṇa recovered the gem and handed it over to Satrājita.

9. Thou art my sole support

O Lord, it is stated that Thou who art gracious to Thy devotees, hast liberated the persons alluded heretofore. And so, I always concentrate my mind on Thy feet. Thou shouldst on Thy part, therefore, say thus to Thyself —"Oh! This one is really in distress. I must therefore, do him a favour and liberate him from his calamities", for Thou art my only support!

Agā praṇatavatsalā! mhaṇati tyā janā pāvalā,
Mhaṇūna tumacyāca mī smaratase sadā pāvalā.
'Karū bari kṛpā, harū vyasana, dīna hā tāpalā'—
Ase mani dharā; kharā bharavasā malā āpalā.

10. Even the Gaṅgā seems to discard me!

On noticing me, the river Gaṅgā which has originated at Thy feet[1] abruptly ejaculates, 'Oh! I have never heard of such a colossal sin that you are!' Saying thus, she presses her hands on her ears, does not even open her eyes and gets terror-stricken! Even though I am keen on seeking my liberation, I would never think of prevailing on her to do me a favour!

Malā nirakhitā bhavaccaraṇakanyakā āpagā,
Mhaṇe, 'agai! aikilehi na kadhi ase pāpa, gā!'
Kara śravaṇi ṭhevite, nughadi netra, ghe bhītilā
Na ghālina bhidesa mī, jarihi kāryalobhī, tilā.

1. *Purāṇas* say that the river Gaṅgā has originated from Lord Viṣṇu's holy feet and its water is supposed to have the power to wash away all kinds of sins.

11. I have worshipped all the deities but in vain!

O Lord, for salvation, I have so often placed my head at the feet of all the deities, that my forehead has permanently become blackavized and stiff but in vain. And so, I see no one now to save me except Thy lotus feet. Even after bestowing on Thy humble devotee the prerogative of final beatitude, Thou goest on saying that Thou art sunk deep in the debt of his devotion! Fie upon the abominable life of a man who does not adore the Lord who is really so gracious to His devotee!

Sadaiva namitā jari pada lalāta kele kiṇe,
Nase itara tāritā maja bhavatpadābjāviṇe.
Natā karuni muktahī, mhaṇasi, 'mī budālo riṇe'.
Aśā tuja na jo bhaje manuja, dhik tayāce jiṇe!

12. God finds me to be a peculiarly greedy beggar

O Lord, perhaps Thou mayest be saying to Thyself, 'I have bestowed on him agile bodily organs, human species, a righteous Brahmin character found very rarely in men[1] besides an aptitude to hear and also to sing the sacred saga of my glory. Still he continues to ask for more and more. It seems, he is a peculiarly avaricious fellow amongst all the mendicants.'

"Paṭutva sakalendriyī, manujatā, suvaṁśī janī,
Dvijatvahi dile bhale, bahu alabhya je kī janī;
Yaśaśravaṇakīrtanī ruci dilī, tarī hā 'varā'
Mhaṇe 'adhika dyāca kī', akhila yācakī hāvarā!"

1. What is rare is not merely a birth in the Brahmin caste, but the truly virtuous Brahmin character which can be found in one belonging to any caste vide *Mahābhārata*, Vana Parva, cantos 180 and 212, 216.

13. Thy favour is still inadequate!

O the Lord of Lakṣmī, magnanimous and affectionate as Thou art, Thou wilt I am sure, never say so. But I thought for a moment that Thou mightest perhaps do so. Therefore, with folded hands, I beg Thy pardon. Sire, it is true that Thou hast bestowed on me so many gifts. But still, Thy favours seem to me inadequate just as a chaste and faithful wife, howsoever, profusely decked with ornaments, would continue to remain care-worn so long as she does not get the company of her spouse!

Ase na mhaṇaśīla tū, varada vatsala, Śrīkarā!
Parantu maja bhāsale, mhaṇuni joḍito mī karā;
Dile bahu bare khare, pari game kṛpā vyaṅga tī,
Alaṅkṛtimatī satī mani jhure, na jo saṅgatī.

14. I only beg for the sight of Thy feet!

O Lord, if Thou wishest to show me compassion to the fullest extent, then only the favours done to me so far will be considered to have really reached me and have become fruitful. But O Hari, let me have the sight of Thy feet as early as possible.[1] And if Thou dost not at all wish to do me this great favour, the gifts conferred on me may be taken back and presented to someone who considers them as valuable. Why give them to me? I am after all a greedy fellow!!

Karāla purati dayā tari aso dile pāvale;
Parantu, Hari! ekadā tvarita dākhavā pāvale,
Prasāda karaṇe manī jari nasela, he āvarā;
Jayā bahu, tayāsa dyā; maja kaśāsa? mī hāvarā!

1. Compare Holy Bible, Old Testament, Psalm 27 (a psalm of David), stanza 4 'One thing have I desired of the Lord, that will I seek after; that I may dwell in the house of the Lord all the days of my life, to behold the beauty of the Lord'.

15. Entrust me to the care of the saints

A disrepute in the public that Thou hast withdrawn Thy gifts is, however, not desirable. As for me, I am sure I shall have an opportunity to see Thy purest feet some day or the other. But at least do me now a favour by entrusting the responsibility of my salvation to Thy dearest saints who would endeavour to discharge it to the best of their abilities. Why shouldst Thou feel humiliated over my proposal?

'Dile phiruni ghetale', aśi akīrti lokī na ho;
Sunirmala tujhī pade kadhi tarī vilokīna, ho!
Nijapriyajanākade tarihi de havālā; jaśī
Padela samajāviśī, taśi karota; kā lājaśī?

16. Punishest me for my impudence!

Alas! I have become so highly impudent as to say to the Supreme Lord that He should not feel humbled over my proposal! But, O the compassionate Lord, at least Thou shouldst not be touchy and get annoyed even though a devotee in an excited state of mind may have become insolent. In any case a grave offence has definitely been committed by me. Therefore, do chastise me because it has been Thy vow to vanquish those who crossing the bounds of righteousness behave in an unrestrained manner!

Ahā! nipaṭa dhṛṣṭa mī prbhuvarāsi 'kā lājaśī?'
Mhaṇe! tuja naso taśī vikṛti, bhāvikālā jaśī,
Parantu aparādha hā guru, mhaṇoni śikṣā karī;
Aseci dharilī nayacyutadamārtha dīkṣā karī.

17. Givest for my faults a room in Thy stomach!

O Lord, I always commit crores of such types of wrongs and also admit of having done so, and while doing thus do not at all feel ashamed of confessing this. I am indeed a brazen fellow in this respect. If there could be no room for crores of my faults in Thy stupendous stomach which easily contains hundreds of crores of worlds[1] how could Thou accommodate the forest-fire[2] which hadst been swallowed by Thee in Thy incarnation as Lord Śrī Kṛṣṇa?

Sadaiva aparādha he racitase ase koṭi, gā!
Svayehi kathito, nase tiḷahi lāja, mī koṭigā;
Ajāṇḍaśatakoṭi jyā udari sarvadā nāndavā,
Na tyāta avakāśa yā, sthala dile tadā kā davā?

1. According to the *Bhāgavata Purāṇa*, X, canto 8, the child Kṛṣṇa once opened his mouth before mother Yaśodā when the latter saw within it all the worlds!
2. There is a story in *Bhāgavata Purāṇa* (X, canto 19) which says that when once a devastating fire broke out in Gokula, Lord Kṛṣṇa swallowed it and protected the cowherds.

18. Let my faults serve as oblation to the forest-fire!

O Lord, Thy stomach hast till now digested numerous wrongs of Thy humble servants who had come to Thee for refuge. But queerly, it now refuses to digest only my blemishes! There must, therefore, be something wrong with me alone. Please offer my faults as an oblation to that hunger-stricken forest-fire! It is a virtue of the sacred rivers of Thy compassion to meet the wishes of Thy dependents by satiating their hunger and thirst!

Tujhyā jiravile bahu praṇatamantu poṭe; paṇa
Tyajī madaparādha he; majakadeci khoṭepaṇa;
Davāgni jaṭharī atikṣudhita, tyāsa he anna dyā;
Vitṛṣṇa karitī śritā tumaciyā dayāsannadyā.

19. Why find my uplift so difficult?

Just as water supports a lotus with ease, similarly the stupendous feat of supporting the three worlds, which none else can achieve, is accomplished by Thy foot with perfect ease and without the least exertion. Why then shouldst Thou find the task of my liberation so tough? O Lord, even common men try their best to relieve their dependants of their hardships and never allow the services rendered by them to become fruitless!

Na hoya kavaṇāhi, te tumaciyāci līlālase
Pade carita dāvije trijagadabjakīlālase;
Maduddharaṇa mātra kā jaḍa tumhā dise? vāritī
Svakavyasana martyahī, na karitīca sevā ritī.

20. O cloud, turn towards the cātaka!

O Lord, if Thou the cloud of mercy movest this way, Thy devotees in the form of cātaka birds[1] would not lack anything whatsoever. For how is it ever possible that the sovereign Lord wouldst neglect His simple and sincere devotees? O the ocean of compassion! It is Thou alone whose heart is moved spontaneously with boundless mercy as soon as Thou beholdest persons in distress having no support other than Thee!

Dayābda vaḷaśīla tū, tari na cātakā sevakā
Uṇe kimapi; bhāvikā ubagaśīla tū deva kā
Ananyagatikā janā nirakhitāci sopadravā
Tujheci, karuṇārṇavā mana dharī umopa dravā.

1. It is said of the bird cātaka that it never drinks ground-water howsoever thirsty it may be and always looks for the drops of rain to fall from the clouds to quench its thirst!

21. I am in the clutches of Kalī!

Kalī initiated a deadly strife with the most righteous king Nala.[1] I after all being obviously immersed in numerous sins, find myself into the close clutches of Kalī like a tiny grasshopper enveloped in a forest-fire! Just as crows in a forest are found ever prepared to prick the heads of cattle to make wounds thereon, in the same way strong worldly passions like enemies have taken positions in my heart to tease and torment me. How would a frog not regard a snake as its very doom?

Kaḷī kari sunirmaḷī parama ugra dāvā Naḷī,
Tayāta aviśuddha mī, śalabha jevi dāvānaḷī;
Vraṇārtha paśucyā śirāvarī vanī ubhe kākase
Smarādi ripu manmanī; ahi na kāḷa bhekā kase?

1. For King Nala, see *Mahābhārata*, Vana Parva, Nalopakhyāna.

22. Kindly sell me for the boat-fare!

O Thou, the boatman in the vast river of this worldly existence, (Bhavamahānadī)[1] I will surely cross it over with Thy help; And Thou mayst then sell off this beggar to the ascetics for recovery of the fare of the boat! I am aware of their life in the hermitage. Therefore, O Lord, dost take pity on me and have an experience of my qualities. Being poor, I am always accustomed to hard work.

Tarena tumacyā baḷe, bhavamahānadīnāvikā!
Tumhīca maga ātarāstava malā sudīnā vikā;
Ase vidita vāsahī maja sadāśramīcā, karā
Dayā, guṇa pahā; save maja sadā śramī cākarā.

---

1. Compare the English poet Pope:
'On life's vast ocean diversely we sail
Reason the card, but passion is the gale'
(Essay on Man; Second Epistle, lines 107/108)
Also H.W. Longfellow:
'Foot-prints that perhaps another,
Sailing over life's solemn main,
A forlorn and ship-wrecked brother
Seeing, shall take heart again.'
—*A Psalm of Life*

23. Even the rich accept mean presents!

What dearth is there of riches and servants in Thy house? Limitless is Thy wealth and a host of servants are in Thy command. And what benefit worth the name would accrue to him who is the lord of jewels, gold and the earth by adding iron to his stock? But please bear in mind that even wealthy and mighty persons do keep all sorts of things, big and small in their stock and willingly accept a thing for whatever it is worth!

Dhanā, parijanā, gharī tumaciyā uṇe kāyase?
Na lābha maṇihemabhūpatisa jodilyā āyase;
Pari prabhuhi saṅgrahī sakala vastulā ṭhevitī,
Guṇā na mhaṇatā uṇāadhika, ādare sevitī.

24. I can equal God Śaṅkara with Thy grace!

Although I now seem to be a simpleton and a poor chap, yet dost Thou think that I would remain a penniless beggar for ever? O Lord, let Thy foot once do me a favour. Thou takest away only for a short while your foot resting on the comely bosom of Goddess Lakṣmī and keepest it on my head. The moment this is done, God Gaṅgādhara[1] will by virtue of my merit find in me a friend of equal status.

Dise, mhaṇuni śāśvataprakṛti raṅka mī kāya? ho!
Prasanna tumacā bare majavarī, prabho, pāya ho.
Kṣaṇa tyajuni Indirābṛhadurojasaṅgā, dharā.
Śirī pada, miḷo sakhā-sama-suśīla gaṅgādharā.

1. Gaṅgādhara is an epithet of Lord Śaṅkara. Lord Śaṅkara holds in his matted locks the river Gaṅgā which has originated from the holy feet of Lord Nārāyaṇa. The poet says, O Nārāyaṇa, if Thou puttest Thy foot on my head, it would get consecrated by the same holy water. Thus my position will get instantly elevated and be on par with that of God Śaṅkara.

25. Teachest this babe how best to sing Thy praise

O Lord, Thou mayest be saying to Thyself—This fellow does not understand how to extol the attributes of great persons. But knowing me as one who loves to be praised, this poor fellow longing earnestly to sing my praise has been in his prattling tones anyhow uttering my name. Sir, how is it possible for a babe to do anything neatly at the very outset? It would, therefore, be proper if Thou Thyself instructest it bit by bit making it in the long run sufficiently enlightened to tread on the right path. (To qualify itself to compose in Thy honour songs befitting Thee.)

> "Prabhustuti na thāukī, pari ticyā mahākāmukā
> Malā kṛpaṇa mārito bahu sakāma hākā mukā."
> Mhaṇā mani ase; kase prathama nīta ye lekarā?
> Haḷūhaḷu paṭu svaye supathi lāviyele karā.

26. A child's prattle is fondly viewed by its father!

It is generally observed that when a child utters letters with its mouth (for instance mamma, dad, papa in prattling tones) its father hears them with rapt earnestness and feels greatly fascinated. He also feels very happy when others appreciate the child's prattle. (In a striking contrast with this, it is seen that) A son will never fail to term his father's talk as 'bitter' if he finds it disagreeable. Such are thus the different ways of the likes and dislikes of men. But O Gracious Nārāyaṇa! of what avail are these instances of common folk to Thee? (These are meaningless since they are not applicable to Thee.)

Janī tari ase ase śiśuhi je mukhe varṇa vī,
Pitā piuni te bhule, madhuratā sukhe varṇavī;
Manā jari na ye, gurūktahi mhaṇe 'kaṭu' prāyaśā;
Dayānidhi! tumhāpuḍhe janakathā aśā kāyaśā?

27. When would poets equal to Thee be born to sing Thy glory?

O Lord Nārāyaṇa! even Brahmadeva[1] who is thoroughly conversant with the quintessence of the Vedas says that Thy greatness is inconceivable and Thy virtues countless! How then is it possible for we people to glorify Thy greatness in the fullest measure? But persons devoted to Thee have by composing hymns in Thy honour according to their capabilities got their hearts cleansed of worldly passions. O Lord! When would poets matching Thee in Thy greatness be born to sing adequately Thy glory?

'Atarkya mahimā tujhā, guṇahi phāra' bā he vidhi
Śṛtijñahi mhaṇe sadā, stavila āmucī kevi dhī?
Tarī jana yathāmati stavuni jāhale sanmatī;
Stavārtha tujhiyā tujhyāsama kavī kadhī janmatī?

1. In *Bhagavata* there is a chapter named 'Brahmastuti' which contains the eulogy by Brahmadeva of Śrı Kṛṣṇa, the complete incarnation of Lord Narāyaṇa.

28. Why should I alone remain unfavoured?

Thou likest self praise and so Thou conferest favours on those who sing Thy praise. And to Thy humble devotees Thou even givest Thy all! This generosity of Thine is known to all those who beg for Thy favours. That is why we go on singing sacred songs of Thy glory as best as we are capable of. O Lord, why should then I alone be denied the fruit of the praises sung by me according to my abilities, so far?

Nijastuti tumhā ruce; staviti tyā vare tarpitā,
Namaskṛtiparā bare svadhana sarvahī arpitā;
Svabhāva tumacā asā vidita jāhalā yācakā;
Karū stava jasātasā; phaḷa navhe janā yāca kā?

29. How much should I praise Thee on Thy face?

O Lord, Thou possessest an extremely pleasing disposition and art the ablest benefactor. I am very poor and helpless and have come to Thee for refuge. I am repeating this so that Thou mayest bear it well in mind. O Lord of the universe, how much should I extol Thy attributes on Thy very face?

Tumhī parama cāṅgale bahusamartha dāte ase;
Sudīna jana mī tumhā śaraṇa āji ālo ase;
Punhāhi kathito bare śravaṇa he karāyāstava;
Samakṣa kiti āpalā, sakalalokarāya! stava?

30. Unlike Thee, saints dislike being praised!

Even some great men shut their ears (to avoid hearing self-praise) as if they feel scorched by these hymns! Thou mayest perhaps ask who these (magnanimous) persons are! I tell Thee that they lie in the dust-particles of Thy feet (and are no other than Thy saints). But it is our good fortune that Thou likest praise even if done in Thy presence! O Thou Nārāyaṇa, the Benefactor, the sea of kindness! how catastrophic it would have been if Śaṅkara had not swallowed the poison?[1] (The poet means to say that if Lord Nārāyaṇa were not to digest this poison of 'eulogy' the sinners would have been left with no chance of liberation!)

Kitī śravaṇa jhākitī prabhuhi, kāya te poḷatī!
Pusāla jari 'koṇa?' te padarajī tujhyā loḷatī;
Bare tujaci sosave stavana, kṛttivāsā garā
Na pī tari kase ghaḍe? hitakarā, dayāsāgarā!

1. When the gods and the demons started churning the sea for obtaining the nectar, the first to come out of the sea was the deadly poison 'Hālāhala' which soon started burning the universe. Lord Śaṅkara, thereupon swallowed the poison and protected the universe. (*Bhāgavata Purāṇa* VIII canto 7)

31. Thou canst digest the poison of praise!

Even though this poison of praise is sweet (for ears) yet as soon as it is taken it makes one arrogant, tarnishes the face of good fame and puts to shame even the deadly poison (digested by God Śaṅkara)! Therefore, O Nārāyaṇa, Thou who art habituated to drinking this unique poison of praise art no doubt more powerful than Śaṅkara; and whosoever dedicates to Thee this poison of praise is rewarded by Thee, in exchange, by a gift of Thy nectar! (liberation).

Gamo madhura he viṣa 'stavana' sevitā mājavī,
Karī malina sadyaśomukha, halāhalā lājavī,
Harāparisa tū barā, prabhuvarā, sadā jo piśī
Asā rasa, samarpityā amṛta āpule opiśī.

32. Thou art consort both of Lakṣmī and Stuti!

O consort of Lakṣmī, who has originated from Kṣīrasāgara as also the consort of 'Stuti' (praise) sprung up from the minds of the renowned poets, the righteous do not accept their own praise for they deem it a sin to do so. O Lord, this (maiden) Stuti on noticing in the saints some of Thy virtues, is for a moment deluded and mistaking their identity for Thine goes on to embrace them. But on her attention being diverted towards Thee, she gets perplexed for a moment, but then recovering herself instantly places herself at Thy service!!

Kavīśvaramanaḥpayonidhisutā stutīcyā pate!
Bhale na varitī stutīprati, na joḍitī pāpa te,
Gaḷā paḍati jyāñciyā tava guṇaikadeśabhrame,
Tihī tujaci dāvitā, bhajati, bā, tulā saṁbhrame.

33. Kindly accept my daughter (poem) as bride!

O Lord, I am therefore dedicating my 'Kavitāsutā'[1] well-bedecked to Thee. O the wearer of golden-coloured clothes, though she does not possess so many virtues, yet she declines to marry anyone else. Therefore, O Hari, kindly treatest her as Thy maid-servant and thus relieve me from her firm resolve to marry only Thee, just as Thou hadst relieved the famous elephant Gajendra from the clutches of the crocodile![2]

Mhaṇoni Kavitāsutā tuja samarpito sājarī;
Nase bahutaśī guṇī, Kanakapītavāsā! jarī,
Tarī na itarā varī; Hari! karī ilā kiṅkarī,
Mayūrahi nijātmajāgrahavimukta, jaisā karī.

1. Kavitāsutā—Daughter in the form of poem.
2. See fn. to verse 6.

34. Thou hadst espoused Satyabhāmā, Thy enemy's daughter!

O Lord, if Thou remembering my faults committed hitherto refusest to accept my daughter (poem), then please listen to what I say. I am no doubt the most unrighteous, but just as Sūrya's friend Satrājita (who had offended Thee) had dedicated his daughter Satyabhāmā to Thee[1] in marriage with great humility, in the same way I am also with folded hands and with humble salutations dedicating my daughter (poem) to Thee!

> Smaroni kṛta mantulā, na kavitāvadhūsvīkṛtī
> Karāla, tari āyakā, prabhu, kharāca mī duṣkṛtī,
> Namaskṛtipurassara svakṛti arpito āji tī,
> Dilī Ravisakhe tumhā jaśi namoni Sātrājitī.

1. After tracing out the 'Syamantaka' gem, Lord Kṛṣṇa handed it over to Satrājita. Satrājita, realising that he had made a false accusation of theft against Śrī Kṛṣṇa and had harassed him unnecessarily, surrendered to him and to redress the wrong done, dedicated his daughter, Satyabhamā to Lord Kṛṣṇa. (See *Harivaṁsha Purāṇa*, canto 38)

35. Thou hadst even accepted Jāmbavanta's ugly daughter

But O Lord, Thou mayest say 'Though the father (Satrājita) was no doubt wicked, yet his daughter Satyabhāmā was virtuous, guiltless and pretty and that is why I had perforce to accept her as my spouse'. I would now request Thee to tell me how the daughter of that quarrelsome, obstinate and ruffianly Jāmbavanta bear who fought with Thee for twenty-seven days and nights, was in appearance?[1] (If Thou could accept her who was so ugly and repulsive to sight how could Thou justifiably then think of declining to accept the fair daughter (poem) of a poor and humble person like me?)

"Pitā khaḷa, parantu ti guṇavatī satī cāṅgalī,
Mhaṇoni maja āpulyā bhajanī lāvaṇe lāgalī."
Mhaṇāla, tari tatsutā kaśī? tumhāsave bhāṇḍagā
Aharniśihi bhāṇḍalā triṇavarātra jo dāṇḍagā.

1. In the course of his search for 'Syamantaka' gem Śrī Kṛṣṇa had to enter a dark cave in which Jāmbavanta the bear had his resort. Jāmbavanta had given the gem to his child to play with. Śrī Kṛṣṇa had to wrestle fiercely with Jāmbavanta continuously for twenty-seven days. Ultimately, Jāmbavanta was defeated and he returned the gem to Śrī Kṛṣṇa. He also dedicated his daughter Jāmbavatī to Śrī Kṛṣṇa to be his spouse. (See Ibid.)

36. Unlike Ahalyā my daughter is spotless!

But O Lord, Thou mayest say that Jāmbavati was fair and that might be said to be proper also. For Thou wouldst have with Thy dexterous hand, which is really a mine of joy, decked her in a way as to be a spouse of your liking. Thou dost indeed possess such a wonderful skill. To quote an instance, Thou hadst by the touch of the dust of Thy feet created the most handsome lady out of a stone![1] But unlike Ahalyā who was cursed by her husband, my piece of work (poem) does not suffer from any such malediction. Further, just as Ahalyā was so pretty as to fascinate Hari (God Indra) and also occupies a place in the category of 'Virtuous Women', likewise my piece of literature (poem) is also so exquisite in composition as to entice Hari (God Viṣṇu) and falls into the class of chaste compositions; yet there is a difference between Ahalyā and my piece of art in that unlike Ahalyā, my work is not tainted with the blemish of sin!

Tilāhi baravī mhaṇā, ucita hoya, toṣākare;
Asela sajalī yathāruci tayī svayoṣā kare;
Jaśī padaraje śilā; pari ase na he śāpilī —
Dhave, Harimanoharākṛti satī aghe vyāpilī.

1. God Indra took fascination for Ahalyā the wife of sage Gautama and masquerading as Gautama went to his hut when he was away and defiled the chastity of Ahalyā. Gautama on knowing about it got enraged over the sin though unwittingly committed by his wife and uttered a curse on her that she would be transformed into a stone. After his anger had subsided he realised that his wife was perfectly chaste and faithful but fell a prey to the fraud practised on her by Indra. Thereupon he pronounced on her उ:शाप (uśśāpa) to the effect that she would revert to her original form when Lord Rāma's feet would touch her. Ahalyā, Draupadī, Sītā, Tārā and Mandodarī are known as the great 'Five Virtuous Women' in Hindu Mythology.

37. Thou hadst favoured even the hump-backed Kubjā!

O Lord, I am reminded of one more instance at this right moment. Didst Thou not restore to normalcy the deformed figure of Kubjā, the hump-backed female servant in the palace of the King Kaṁsa, by a touch of Thy hand[1] which is a repository of the particles of the purest nectar of compassion? Am I such a pariah that Thou shouldst favour even the hump-backed female servant of Thy enemy but dislike my poetic piece of work so much so that Thou shouldst not even think of improving upon it and making it elegant to suit Thy taste?

Bhale smaraṇa jāhale samayi; kaṁsadāsī kare
Kaśī ujaralī, samujjvaladayāsudhāsīkare?
Tumhā svaripucī taśī baṭika āvaḍe, matkṛtī
Nako, na sajave, asā bahuta kāya mī duṣkṛtī?

1. Kubjā was the hump-backed female servant in the palace of King Kaṁsa. There is a legend that when Kṛṣṇa and Balarāma went to Mathurā, she applied a paste of scented sandalwood to them. Kṛṣṇa was very much pleased with her and rectified the deformity in her figure by the touch of his hand! (*Bhāgavata Purāṇa* X, cantos 42, 48)

38. Thou hadst relished Vidura's coarse-flour wheat dish!

O the Āptakāma, may this poetical work of mine receive Thy approbation just as the handful of 'Pohe'[1] presented to Thee by Sudāmā had received Thine. Even though Thou rollest in riches, Thou art very courteous and also very near and dear to us (devotees). Why wouldst Thou then behave so curtly with us? It is said that Thou hadst very much relished Vidura's 'Kaṇyā'[2] and partook of it to Thy heart's content. If this be true, why did he at all offer that poor dish of Kaṇyā to Thee, his Lord and whom he regarded as his very soul?

Jaśī pṛthukatandulaprasṛti, āptakāmā taśī
Ruco kṛti; sabhāgya tū sunaya āpta kā mātaśī?
Kaṇyā Viduramandirī mhaṇati sādhu āsvādilyā;
Khare jari, kaśā tuja prabhusi āpulyā svā dilyā?

1. Sudāmā, a poor Brahmin, was Kṛṣṇa's chum. When he came to meet Kṛṣṇa, he brought with him a handful of Pohe (flattened type of rice) as a present for Kṛṣṇa who relished them heartily.
2. Vidura a very virtuous non-royal character in the *Mahābhārata*, was like an uncle to the Pāṇḍavas and Kauravas. When Lord Kṛṣṇa went to Hastināpura on behalf of the Pāṇḍavas to hold the final peace talks so as to avoid the deadly war, he (Kṛṣṇa) during his stay at Hastināpura refused the rich royal entertainments offered by Duryodhana, and instead preferred the coarse food at Vidura's residence. (*Mahābhārata*, Udyoga Parva, canto 91)

39. Thou hadst even accepted Śabarī's berries!

O Lord, Śabarī had bitten the berries with her loose teeth to taste if they were delicious and had also taken them close to her nose to make sure if they smelt sweet before offering them to Thee![1] (And Thou too had relished them heartily!) Now leave aside this old story. Better have a general review of the saga of Thy glory (and Thou wouldst come across a number of such instances).

Jiṇe rasa pahāvayā praśithilī radī cāvilī,
Suvāsahi kaḷāvayā prathama nāsikī lāvilī,
Tumhāsi śabarī taśī badarikāphaḷe de; junī
Kathā aśī aso, pahā svacarite tumhī mejunī.

1. Śabarī was a female 'Bhilla' (a race of forest-dwellers). When Rāma and Lakṣmaṇa were staying in the forest during the period of their exile, they once visited Śabarī's hut. She was extremely happy to see them and received them by presenting a handful of berries. But before doing so, she tasted the berries herself to make sure that they were sweet. Lord Rāma ate them with great pleasure and conferred on her 'Mokṣapada" (liberation). (*Adhyātma Rāmāyaṇa*, Araṇya Kāṇḍa)

40. We must surrender to Thee to get Thy favours

O Lord, thou art never unjust to anybody once he completely surrenders himself to Thee! The best thing, therefore, for a man to do in his own interest, is to give himself up fully to Thee! It is true that whenever Thou desirest to bless anyone Thou dost it at once without a moment's delay; yet if the bird Cātaka were not to keep its beak open, how could the drops of rain fall into its mouth?[1]

Prabho! śaraṇa āliyāvari na vhā kadhī vākaḍe,
Mhaṇoni itukeci he svahitakṛtya jīvākaḍe;
Prasāda karitā nase paḷa vilamba, bāpā, khare;
Ghanāmbu na paḍe mukhī ughadilyāvinā pākhare.

1. Compare the English proverb, 'God helps those who help themselves'. Also Tagore — 'Life of my life, I shall ever try to keep all untruths out of my heart, knowing that Thou art that Truth which has kindled the light of reason in my mind. I shall ever try to drive all evils away from my heart and keep my love in flower knowing that Thou hast Thy seat in the inmost shrine of my heart. (*Gitāñjali*)

41. I am still steeped in worldly pleasures!

O Lord, Thy kind feet are never contaminated with the blemish of hard-heartedness. We men commit mistakes, but it is Thou who givest us protection. I have not surrendered myself to Thee in true spirit, for I have not still got rid of the worldly passions completely. Those who have the fortune to taste the nectar (of Thy grace) would never think of taking the wine! (of worldly pleasures).

Śive na tujhiyā padā adayatākhya doṣa kṣaṇa;
Prabho, cukataso, tarī karisi tūci saṁrakṣaṇa;
Naseci śaraṇāgatī ghaḍali satya adyāpi tī;
Ruce viṣaya; jyā miḷe amṛta, te na madyā pitī.

42. I pray to Thee to forgive me like Ajāmiḷa.

O Lord, unmindful of the consequences, I have deliberately and openly committed numerous sins of various kinds. So I now surrender myself to Thee who art the very bridge on the unsurmountable 'River of Woe' and beseech unto Thee thus, 'O Lord, in the pursuit of sinful ways, I am just a companion of Ajāmiḷa.[1] Kindly forgive me too.

Vipāka na gaṇoni, myā prakaṭa āpulyā ghātake
Kaḷoni, amite baḷe vividha joḍilī pātake;
'Kṣamasva bhagavannajāmilasakho, smi' aise tulā
Mhaṇe namuniyā sudustaravipannadīsetulā.

1. For Ajāmiḷa, see note under verse 2. Compare, Old Testament, Psalm 25, stanza 7 'Remember not the sins of my youth, nor my transgressions; according to Thy mercy remember Thou me for Thy goodness' sake O Lord'. Also Psalm 27 quoted above under verse 14: 'Hear O Lord, when I cry with my voice; have mercy also upon me, and answer me' (Stanza 7). Also Aurobindo, 'The soul goes to the Mother-Soul in all its desires and troubles, and the Divine Mother wishes that it should do so, so that She may pour out her heart of love.' ('The Synthesis of Yoga', Part III Chapter 3, p. 544)

43. I would then call Thee really all-powerful!

O Lord, it is not untrue but a perfect truth that Thou who hadst subdued the pride of God Indra and art the doer of splendidly generous deeds, hadst held the (Govardhana) hill on the palm of Thy hand.[1] But if Thou couldst lift me up who am a horrid sinner from the mire of sin, then only I shall surely name Thee as the unique hero in all the three worlds!!

Navhe anṛta, satya, te, acala ūcalīlā kare
Tuvā Harimadāpahe, bṛhadudāralīlākare;
Samuddharasi ekaṭā jari jaḍāsi yā kardamī;
Mhaṇena bhuvanatrayī tari tulā 'bhalā marda' mī.

1. See fn. to verse 5.

44. A physician is great to a patient whom he cures!

Even though a man might be renowned as a 'very successful physician' and might have also completely rooted out the tree of diseases of many a patient, yet so long as that physician has not fully exterminated an extremely unendurable enemy in the form of the disease of a particular patient, that poor fellow at least, will not believe in the proficiency of the physician!

Cikitsaka 'bhalā bhalā' mhaṇuni phāra vakhāṇilā,
Jarī bahujanāmayadṛma samūlahī khāṇilā,
Tathāpi atiduḥsahasvagadaśatrucyā atyayā —
Vinā na hṛdayī dharī saruja pāmara pratyayā.

45. May I remain ever impatient for Thy favours!

O Lord, Thou mayest, if Thou likest, dub me impatient, but I think by doing so, Thou hast indicated my virtue only and O Lord who bestowest bliss on Thy devotees as a cloud gives extreme delight to a peacock, may my mind always remain similarly impatient for Thee! All the worldly display including our lives, seems to be transient;[1] our mind is not certain of what may happen at any moment and hence goes on rotating like a wheel as a result of the innumerable worries. Why then should I not become impatient for Thy grace?

Mhaṇā maja utāviḷā, guṇaci ghetalā, ghābare
Aso mana aseci, bā bhajakabarhimeghā, bare;
Dise kṣanika sarva he, bharavasā ghaḍicā kase
Dharīla mana? ādhine bahu paribhrame cākase.

1. Compare Shakespeare
'Out, out brief candle!
Life is but a waking shadow, a poor player,
That struts and frets his hour upon the stage,
And then is heard no more.....' (*Macbeth*)
Also, for our mind goes on rotating like a wheel as a result of innumerable worries, compare James Montegomery,
'The world's a wilderness of woe
And life's a pilgrimage of pain.'

46. Being decrepit I am obliged to become impatient!

Old age which is, as it were, the white flag of Yama's army (in the form of gray hair) has come within the range of my sight. While fighting with the diseases which are like the vanguard of Yama's forces, this body is thoroughly exhausted. O Lord, there is none in my view mightier than Thou who could come to my rescue. And, therefore, when my enemy is on the point of chopping off my neck,[1] what else can I do but to become impatient?

Kṛtāntakaṭakāmaladhvajajarā diso lāgalī,
Puraḥsaragadāsave jhagaḍatā tanū bhāgalī;
Sahāya dusarā nase tujaviṇe baḷe āgaḷā;
Na ho jari utāviḷā, svaripu kāpito hā gaḷā.

1. Compare H.W. Longfellow
'Art is long and Time is fleeting
And our hearts though stout and brave,
Still, like muffled drums are beating
Funeral marches to the grave.'
—*A Psalm of Life*

47. Savest me while there is good time!

O Lord, it is Thy bounden duty to protect Thy humble devotee which Thou must discharge unfailingly. Why then this unnecessary delay? And how long should I, a poor and feeble person continue to spend the days of my life in lamenting and moaning? However, it does not behove Thee to run down all alone.[1] So it would be in the fitness of things if Thou liberatest me in time so long as Yama has not laid his hand on me.

Avaśya karaṇe khare praṇatarakṣaṇa svocita,
Uśira maga kā? baso kṛpaṇa mīhi kā śocita?
Navhe prabhuvarā! tumhā ucita ekaṭe dhāvaṇe,
Kṛtānta śivalā nase, tava dise bare pāvaṇe.

1. To run down to the help of a person in his last hour without the accompaniment of Thy requisite paraphernalia befitting to Thy glory and power.

48. My good condition would be creditable also to Thee!

Perhaps Thou mayest say, 'I shall protect you anyhow and fulfil all your desires. Why should you worry about me?' But O Lord, who art our most beloved and the very life of the universe, in the plenitude and prosperity of the forest lies the well-being of the animals taking resort therein.[1]

'Kase tari karū tujhe avana, pūravū āḷa jī
Asela mani; āmucī tuja kaśāsa re kāḷajī?'
Ase jari mhaṇāla, ho priyatamā, jagajjīvanā!
Tadāśritamṛgāsi tī sukhasamṛddhi, bā, jī vanā.

1. The prosperity of the place of shelter is reflected in the well-being of the person taking shelter therein; if the protector is dismal or unhappy, the same would be the state of his dependant too. That is the universal rule.

49. Thou art the support of our lives!

A child finds happiness in the happiness of its mother. And O Lord, who art dearest to us of all our near and dear ones, if a mother is unhappy, the child is bound to be so. Therefore, O Lord, Thou who art our very life need not suffer any kind of hardship even for a moment! Thou art the bridge enabling the people to cross the sea of misery and art verily the support of their lives!

Sukheci sukh bālakā prakaṭa hoya māteciyā;
Tilā ghaḍati je śrama, priyajanottamā! teci yā!
Mhaṇoni na śivo paḷa-kṣaṇahi kaṣṭa, jīvā! tulā,
Vipajjaladhisetulā, sakalalokajīvātulā.

50. Leadest us on to righteousness

O Lord, may we, Thy devotees, be divested of the days of our lives in this world and may such aggregate period go to lengthen Thy span of life![1] For after all, what moral merit worth the name has a weakling like me (and others like me) earned by remaining alive for such a long period?[2] O my beloved friend! mayest Thou be happy for ever and lead the human beings along the righteous path through the darkness of ignorance.[3] O Lord! in this alone lies my gratification.

Asota tuja āmucī sakala bhāvukāyurbaḷe;
Jagoni bahu kāya myā sukṛta joḍile durbaḷe?
Ase, priyatamā! sukhī bahutakāla; māyātamī —
Janā supatha dākhavī, mudita, sattamā, yāta mī!

---

1. Though it may appear incongruous for a devotee to express his willingness to dedicate his life to God (who is in fact immortal) and to wish him long life, the feeling of the poet of his complete surrender to the Almighty has to be appreciated. The poet's readiness to surrender his life to God could be viewed as his humble worship analogous to one's oblation to the river Gaṅgā with its own water!
2. For the wish to surrender one's life to God expressed in the first half of the verse, compare:
   'Take my life, and let it be
   Consecrated, Lord! to thee;
   Take my moments and my days
   Let them flow in ceaseless praise....'
   (F.R. Havergal, quoted in 'Daily Strength for Daily Needs' selected by Mary W. Tileston, p. 295)
3. 'Lead the human beings along the righteous path through the darkness of ignorance' compare
   'Lead, kindly Light amid the encircling gloom,
   Lead Thou me on,
   The night is dark and I am far from home,
   Lead Thou me on.'(J.H. Newman)

51. None is as merciful as Thou art.

Those who would like to say that they have heard lacs of beings in the categories of gods, demons, and men (e.g. Śaṅkara, Prahlāda, Vālmiki) to be like that (merciful), let them do so. But, O Lord, to my mind there is none who is as compassionate as Thou. Thou art still displaying the sign of the kick of sage Bhṛgu's foot on Thy chest[1] (with great pride and joy as if it were a mark of respect!). Poets are imbibing (singing) Thy glorious saga which is unique and pure as nectar, with great earnestness, even today.

> 'Bhale pariśile surāsuranarī tase lakṣa mī,'
> Mhaṇota mhaṇaṇāra, bā; tuja asā nasela kṣamī,
> Urī bhṛgupadāhatī miravitosi adyāpi tī,
> Kavī tava yaśaḥkathā navasudhānavadyā pitī.

1. With a view to ascertain who among the three Gods, Brahmā, Viṣṇu and Maheśa excelled in the virtues of munificence, forbearance and composure, the sage Bhṛgu once approached each one of them turn by turn. He first went to Brahmadeva but did not give him reverential salutation or obeisance due to him. Brahmā felt offended and was enraged. The same thing happened with Śaṅkara also. Bhṛgu thereafter went to Lord Nārāyaṇa in Vaikuṇṭha. Nārāyaṇa was then asleep. Bhṛgu kicked him in his chest. Nārāyaṇa suddenly got up and without getting angry with Bhṛgu started pressing his feet saying, 'Sire, I have really committed a grave offence in that I kept on sleeping when you came to me and did not receive you with due respect. You have done right in chastising me for my omission. Please let me press your foot for a while which may have sustained injury.' Bhṛgu was pleased and said, 'O Nārāyaṇa, you are doubtless great amongst all the Gods, in forgiveness, generosity and serenity! (*Bhāgavata Purāṇa* X-89)

52. We are devoted to Thee in spite of our involvement in worldly things

O Lord, Thou mayest be saying to Thyself, 'If you really have so much fascination for me, why does your mind then abstain from singing and hearing my saga and remains attached to the objects such as your wife, wealth, etc., of this world?' In reply to this objection of Thine, I may well ask Thee how didst Thy mother Yaśodā while engaged in breast feeding Thee, abruptly set Thee aside from her lap (on noticing the milk on the hearth overflowing) and rushed towards the milk? (Would it be proper to conclude from this that the milk was dearer to her than Thou? Certainly not!) (Refer *Bhāgavata Purāṇa*, X 9-5)

"Bhavanmatisa āvade jari dhanādikālāgi te,
Madīya guṇakīrtanaśravaṇa kā tari tyāgite?"
Asehi mhaṇaśila, bā, jari, tarī tujhī māvalī
Tuja tyajuni pājitā, kaśī dudhākaḍe dhāvalī?

53. Kindly free us from the witch of worldly passions!

O Lord, that which induces a person to behave thus, entices his mind and never leaves its hold, namely a craving for enjoyment of worldly objects, is a very powerful sorceress indeed! Therefore, O the omniscient, I beseech Thee to drive her out and then if Thou wouldst ask me to sing Thy glories with a sincere heart, I shall certainly comply.

Anāvara piśācikā viṣayavāsanā satya, jī
Ase karavi kṛtya, jī bhulavite kadhī na tyajī;
Mhaṇoni tuja jāṇatyā vinavito, ilā kāḍha, gā!
Karina maga tū jarī mhaṇasi, 'āpaṇā gādha gā.'

54. She-ass of worldly passions is intractable for householders

O Lord, the stories of Thy sacred life are verily the wish-yielding cows. But a she-ass in the form of the passion for worldly objects, gets mixed up amongst them. It fears none as it fears the cowherd (also means one having control over one's senses) named Śuka,[1] the sage. Persons carrying staffs in their hands try to drive it away but it kicks them off. How could it then be least afraid of one like me who is without a staff?[2] (not an ascetic but an householder).

Tujhyā guṇakathā mahāsurabhi, tyāta hī rāsabhī
Śire viṣayavāsanā; jaśī Śukā ahirāsa bhī
Taśī na itarāsa bhī; isa sadaṇḍahī hākitī,
Tathāpi bahu lāthaḷī; maga adaṇḍa mī hā kitī?

1. Sage Vyasa's son Śuka, a lifelong celibate, had absolute control over all carnal desires.
2. An ascetic is enjoined to keep a staff with him. The number of staffs with the ascetics denotes their particular order, viz, Ekadaṇḍī, Dwidaṇḍī and Tridaṇḍī.

55. Only Thou canst kill the she-ass of worldly passions

Like the demon Khara of Lord Rāma's times, this sensual desire is a Kharī and it is Thou alone who hast the power to put her to death. Even Bakī (Pūtanā) may be said to be good-natured as compared to her. Tāṭaka of Śrī Rāma's period was no doubt a devil but was too mild in her comparison. This Kharī is neither upright nor commonplace. Please dost not entertain any hesitation in totally eliminating her. Be resolute and act. Mayest this be treated as one of the deeds done by Thee in Gokula.[1]

Kharāsura jasā, taśī viṣayavāsanā he kharī;
Hicā vadha karāvayā tujaci śakti āhe kharī;
Bakī sumati, tāṭakā laghu, na he bhalī; lājaśī
Ugāci; taśī eka hī, vrajavanāta līlā jaśī.

1. Like the killing of Pūtanā etc.

56. Destroy this villainous Kharī!

Let all that be now left aside. In order to keep Thy vow, it is incumbent on Thee to ward off, of Thy own accord, the calamities befalling those who come to Thee for refuge. Undoubtedly, it is Thy prime duty. Therefore, O Lord, kindly honour Thy pledge. Was the wickedness of that Khara more dreadful than Kharī's? (No, certainly not). Dost, therefore, give her a decent burial!

Kase tari aso maga; svapaṇarakṣaṇākāraṇe
Avaśya śaraṇāgatavyasana to svaye vāraṇe;
Tumhā vihita mukhya he; na pusatā karā ho! kharī —
Nijokti; khara kāya to adhika? saṁharā ho kharī.

57. To kill Kharī will not be blameworthy

O God, see how tremendously she seeks to influence and tempt Thy devotees! There is in fact nothing wrong or blameworthy in putting her to death, for she is an embodied pest to the saints and ascetics! This Kharī in the form of sensual desires says, 'It is true that the stories depicting the glories of Gods are just like Kāmadhenu in that like the latter's milk which is nourishing, plentiful and sweet, the feeling of devotion generated by the former is capable of leading men to salvation. But when I am your own (and can offer you all pleasures) what is the use in forsaking me and running after milking another's cow?'[1]

> Kharī karitase kaśī tava janīki sattā, pahā;
> Icā vadha na nindya, bā, prabaḷa mūrta sattāpa hā;
> Kathāsurabhicā rasa svahita, puṣkaḷa, svāduhī,
> Mhaṇe, 'tyajuni kā malā nijadhanā parasvā, duhī'?

1. Regarding the devil's temptations to the righteous devotees of God, compare Satan tempting Jesus, New Testament, St. Matthew, Chapter 4 : 'Again, the devil taketh him up into an exceeding high mountain, and sheweth him all the kingdoms of the world, and the glory of them; and saith unto him, All these things will I give thee, if thou wilt fall down and worship me. Then saith Jesus unto him, Get thee hence, Satan: for it is written, Thou shalt worship the Lord thy God, and him only shalt thou serve.

58. Thy saga is more endearing than a mother!

O Lord, the Kāmadhenus in the form of the stories of Thy incarnation period seem to be more affectionate than even a mother, because at the sight of children as also the old, their hearts begin to overflow with the juice of love! Anyone may come and milk them; yet they do not withhold the flow of their milk. The Kāmadhenu by licking the dirt from the body of her calf keeps it clean. The sagas of Thy glory similarly destroy the sins of Thy devotees, but unlike the Kāmadhenu which becomes impure while cleaning her calf, Thy stories never incur any blemish whatsoever!

Kathāsurabhi yā bhalyā svajananīhunī vāṭatī;
Śiśūsa jaraṭhāsahī nirakhitā rase dāṭatī;
Duhota bhalate sadā tari na leśahī āṭatī;
Svavatsamala bhakṣitī, pari na sarvathā bāṭatī.

59. Am I wrong in comparing Thy saga to a cow?

O Lord, I have compared the stories of Thy glory to the Kāmadhenu (Divine Cow) and this seems to me appropriate. But I think I must be truly dull, because the good souls would feel offended on hearing this simile, for even though the stories are undoubtedly exquisite it would not at all be proper to compare them to an animal! Shame be, therefore, to me for, being impudent I have dared to draw such a totally unbecoming comparison without caring to pay any heed to the counsel of these wise men.

Kathāsi upamā dilī surabhicī, dise nīta tī;
Parantu bahumanda mī, mhaṇuni sachṛtī vītatī;
Kathā nirupamā, tayāprati paśūpamā śuddha te —
Navheci; na vicārile budhajanāsi myā uddhate.

60. God likes to be praised!

(I admit I have failed to consult these wise men but) These very wise preceptors tell me a secret quintessence that 'Thou likest Thy praise irrespective of who does it or how he does it and that Thou overlookest the faults of Thy devotee who prays to Thee with a sincere heart.' I, therefore, adore Thee in my own humble way whom the Vedas themselves have eulogised. However, at the same time, I feel unnerved to think how my adoration might be viewed by the erudite authorities!

> Asehi upadeśitī guru rahasya mandā, 'ruce
> Nijastava jasātasā, aguṇa ghe na vandāruce',
> Mhaṇoni nigamastutā bhalatase tulā vānito,
> Parantu hṛdayī mahājanabhayāsa mī mānito.

61. When shall the praises sung by me become faultless?

O Lord, I have always been saying to myself, 'when shall my descriptions attain such a complete perfection that there would not be a single flaw in any of the letters of my devotional poems composed in Thy honour'? Really, I earnestly wish this to transpire. Therefore, O my Lord Hari who art the 'Kalpataru' of Thy devotees, why dost Thou not give me an honourable treatment? I am not afraid in the least to say so, for the truth is afraid of none!

Mhaṇe — 'svakṛticyā uṇe kimapi eka varṇī na ho;
Ase tuja kadhi bare vigataśaṅka varṇina ho!'
Aseci aśi āvaḍī, kariśi kā na atyādara?
Svabhaktasurapādapā! Hari! naseci satyā dara.

62. Kindly makest my mind stable

O God, the child Dhruva fervently desired to adore Thee and so (on noticing the purity and sincerity of his heart) Thou fulfilled his desire lovingly by touching the conch-shell in Thy hand to his cheek.[1] Please treatest me likewise. O the Lord of Lakṣmi, kindly placest Thy lotus-like hand on my head. O the omnipotent God, who conferest a boon on and givest a solemn word of protection to Thy devotees, dost make my mind steady which is sceptical and perplexed!

Dhṛva stavani āvadī dhari, mhaṇoni atyādare
Tumhi karuni dāvili, śivuni galla, satyā, dare;
Tase maja karā, karāmbuja dharā śirī, māvarā!
Varābhayaparā! parākramapaṭo! manā āvarā.

1. The child Dhruva was very keen on eulogizing God, but did not know how to do it. Lord Nārāyaṇa knowing the innocence of the child gave him *Darśana* (became visible) and touching the conch-shell to its cheek conferred on it proficiency in speech. (*Bhāgavata Purāṇa*, VIII-9)

63. Elevatest this poor man by any means possible!

O Lord, let my supplication to Thee to place Thy lotus-like hand on my head be kept aside for I being devoid of any virtue surely do not deserve it. Gods as also reputed wise men pay their homage at Thy feet. (How can then I who am a poor and ignorant person be worthy for the touch of Thy hand?) Even a particle of dust of Thy feet is capable of becoming a place of adoration for all the Three worlds! But, O God, who art reputed to bestow Thy grace, kindly uplift me by whatever means Thou deemest fit, and that is all what I desire!

Karāmbuja aso; nase ucita tyāsa mi pāmara;
Praṇāma karitī padāpratihi sanmatī sāmara;
Padābjarajahī jagattrayanamaskriyābhājana;
Prasādacaturā, kasā tari karā barā hā jana.

64. O Lord, liberatest me like Dhruva

O Lord, Thou hast by the touch of Thy conch-shell uplifted Dhruva. If Thou hast lovingly thought of elevating me likewise, kindly doest so. Doest as Thou thinkest proper. But I do not at all deserve to be treated on par with Dhruva. How lofty he was! By the dint of his unflinching devotion for God, he attained such a unique status that even God Indra should bow to him!

Tumhī karuni dāvilā Dhṛva kṛtārtha jaisā dare,
Taseci jari yojile tumaciyā mane sādare,
Aso; vihita te karā; pari barobarī tyāsave —
Nase ucita; to mahāprabaḷa vandije vāsave.

65. Thou dost not differentiate between the high and the low

How small was Dhruva, but what a rigorous penance had he undergone! And how profound was his faith in Thee! Dhruva was indeed resolute as his name itself indicates. His reputation was so great that he deserved praise of the whole universe. How then dost Thou compare a trifling mustard seed (like me) with the gigantic mountain Meru? (like Dhruva). But O Lord Hari, when once Thou decidest to confer Thy favours, Thou dost not make any distinction whatsoever between the great and the small (supplicants).

Kitī vaya, kase tapa prakhara, kāya viśvāsa to?
Dhṛva dhṛva kharā; stavā ucita hoya viśvāsa to;
Kaśī tuḷitasā tumhī prakaṭa meruśī moharī?
Prasāda karitā uṇe adhika nāṭhavā, ho Harī!

66. Favour should elevate the recipient to the donor's status

But O Lord, real magnanimity after all lies only in such a generous outlook. A gift is to be given with great kindness and in such a manner that on receiving it, the recipient who has become humble at the feet of the donor should attain a status equal to that of the latter. Of what avail is a gift which does not dispel the inferiority of the recipient! O God Rāma, (Lord Nārāyaṇa's incarnation), dost Thou not remember Bibhiṣaṇa, Rāvaṇa's brother? (By doing him a favour didst Thou not elevate him as the king of Laṅkā thereby equalizing his status to Thine as the king of Ayodhyā?)

Prabhutva tari heca kī karuni de kṛpā dāna te,
Svasāmya yadupārjane miravije svapādānate;
Prasāda maga kāya to, jari nivārinā lāghavā?
Kase daśamukhānujā visaralā? aho Rāghavā!

67. Givest me only that which I am worth!

O Lord, kindly be merciful on this servant whose exterior may be rough and rugged but whose interior is perfectly pure, and confer on him a boon which he can readily digest (which he truly deserves). Boons even if lavishly conferred become fruitless if the supplicant is unable to digest them. Therefore, O Lord, kindly see my worth and then only give whatever is commensurate with my merit.

Aso vari kasā tarī, vimala bhāva jyācā karā
Tayāvari dayā; pace vara asāci dyā cākarā;
Vṛthāci gamate dile, bahuhi, je na dāsā jire
Pusoni adhikāra dyā; sukara te sadā sājire.

68. Be discreet in bestowing Thy favours!

O Lord, it seems that Thou art willing to do me a lot of favour. But kindly be discreet, and let not Thine heart be perplexed while granting the boon as happened with God Śiva, who while conferring a boon on a devotee allowed him to become insolent.[1] Let not my disposition become similarly unrighteous. O Lord, how did the fact that Bhasmāsura was a wicked and treacherous demon and that bestowing on him boons lavishly was not advisable, escape, notice of God Śaṅkara? Fortunately, however, Śaṅkara who is a wizard of that dreadful snake of this worldly life was saved by Thee very tactfully.

Prasanna bahu hotasā, pari karāla ho! bāvare —
Śivāpari varāsave hṛdaya, he na ho bā vare;
Asā vṛka kṛtaghna he na kaḷale kase ho Harā?
Bhalā jagavilā tumhī bhavamahāhicā moharā.

1. Pleased with the penance of the demon Vṛka (or Bhasmāsura) Lord Śaṅkara bestowed on him a boon to the effect that anyone on whose head he would place his hand stood to be reduced to ashes! Having become arrogant with the power of the boon, Bhasmāsura in order to become the Lord of Kailāsa thought of experimenting the boon on Śaṅkara himself! On that occasion Lord Nārāyaṇa assuming the form of Mohini (in some texts, the form is referred to as of a Brahmin lad) captivated Bhasmāsura with his enticing talk so much that drunk with mirth he began to dance and while doing so placed his hand on his own head, unawares, with the result that the devil was reduced to ashes the very next moment! (Refer *Bhāgavata*, X-88)

69. Favour only the deserving!

A Brahmin's son named Upamanyu[1] prayed to Thee with an unflinching determination to secure milk for himself. And O Lord Śaṅkara, the slayer of Madana,[2] Thou gavest him a sea of milk itself! A gift could be called judicious if it confers happiness on a really deserving person.[3] But to oblige a villain is like feeding milk to a serpent which invariably becomes a cause for trouble!

Bhaje sudṛdhaniścaye dvijakumāraka kṣīradhī,
Tayā kari tumhīca dyā, madanamāraka! kṣīradhī;
Udārapaṇa te bare, sukhavi je supātrā sadā;
Dile amṛta pannagā, taśi khaḷī kṛpā trāsadā.

1. Upamanyu, a poor Brahmin lad fervently prayed to God Śaṅkara to provide him with milk. Śaṅkara was so much moved by the sincerity of the lad that He created a sea of milk for him! (*Mahābhārata*, Anuśāsana Parva, canto 14)
2. The legend is that Lord Śaṅkara burnt with the flame emerging out of His third eye, Madana, the god of love who had come to enchant Him!
3. Compare *Gītā*, '*des'e kāle ca pātre ca taddānaṁ Sāttvikaṁ Smṛtam* XVII-20'.

70. O the cloud of joy, mayest Thou not discard this peacock!

O Lord Śambho, Thou who art a cloud of joy hast been, from the beginning, very dear and pleasing to the heart of this peacock (Mayūra or Mora; meaning also Moropanta—poet's name). Therefore, Thy compassion may not forsake me even for a moment. In fact I have praised only Thy munificence. Sire, how can a beloved child deliberately make a fun of its elders? Kindly keep in mind that I am verily a simpleton!

Atipriya, sukhaprada, prathama tū mudaṁbhoda, yā —
Mayūrahṛdayā, tujhī kṣana viṭo na, Śambho! dayā;
Udārapaṇa vānile; aji! gurūpahāsā baḷe
Kase karila lekarū? nipaṭa he pahā sābaḷe.

71. Hari and Hara are not different!

O Lord, those who see a distinction between Thou and God Śiva, let them do so. But the wise say that in reality there is no such difference. Therefore, I think that what the Śaivas assert as their belief (viz. that Śaṅkara is superior to Viṣṇu) is not true. Similarly, the Vaiṣṇavas too rigidly stick to their own view unnecessarily. Both these deities are supereminent (equal and similar).

Tumhā Hari Harāta jyā disatase, diso; vāstava,
Prabuddha mhaṇatī, nase tiḷahi bheda; mī yāstava —
Mhaṇe mani, yathārtha je svamata varṇitī śaiva te —
Na; vaiṣṇava durāgrahi, parama mukhya hī daivate.

72. I adore Śaṅkara and Nārāyaṇa alike!

O Lord, at one moment I address my prayer to Purāntaka[1] (Śaṅkara) and at another to Murāntaka that is, to Thee, O Nārāyaṇa. If, therefore, Thou likest to label me as sycophant, then Thou mayest do so without any hesitation. That Śiva adores Thee and Thou worshipest Śiva is the truth revealed by Śuka and Vyāsa. These are legends being narrated since ancient times and are not a present-day fiction. Thou hast, therefore, to hear them patiently. (Allow me to narrate them.)

Mhaṇe kṣaṇa Purāntaka, kṣaṇa Murāntaka; brāhmaṇā —
Malā jari mhaṇāla bā! tari viśaṅka lubrā mhaṇā;
Tumhā Śiva, Śivā tumhī bhajatasā; śuka vyāsa hā —
Sadartha vadale; purātana kathā, na navyā, sahā.

1. Regarding Purantaka (or Tripurantaka, i.e. Destroyer of Tripura), an appellation of God Śiva, see *Harivaṁśa* Bhaviṣya Parva, canto 133.

73. Vyāsa does not forget Thee even in his sleep!

O Lord, Vyāsa,[1] the son of Parāśara is indeed Thy incarnation! His maxims are treated as authoritative by one and all. O Lord of the Three worlds, even though he happens to be disturbed in his sleep yet it is only Thy sacred Nāmāvalī, which like a mother looks after the people with affection and makes them happy by securing salvation for them, that comes out from his mouth!!

Tujhāci avatāra to suta Parāśarācā; vaḷe —
Taduktisa jana; prabho, jari nijemadhe cāvaḷe,
Tarī, tribhuvaneśvarā, tava viśuddha nāmāvalī —
Mukhī prakaṭa hoya, jī kari sukhī janā māvalī.

1. Regarding Vyāsa as an incarnation of Lord Viṣṇu, see *Harivaṁśa*, Harivaṁśa Parva, 41-161.

74. Thy name burns all our sins

O Lord, it is only gradually that our mind becomes capable of assimilating Thy beneficial name. Even an intractable and devilish Kali trembles in his sleeves on hearing Thy name! Thy name not only wipes out all obstacles and sins but also enables its adorer to see Thee, the Lord of Yogamāyā,[1] in person, as had happened in the case of Prahlāda, son of Kayādhū!

Tujhe kuśala nāma bā haḷu haḷū manā ākaḷī
Duratyaya asā mahākhalahi tyāsa bhī hā kaḷī;
Harī Vyasana pāpa he; bahu kaśāsa? kāyādhavā —
Pari tvarita bheṭavī tujahi, yogamāyādhavā.

1. Yogamāyā or Mūla Prakṛti: means the primeal nature which the Nirguṇa and Nirākāra Parabrahma first created when It thought of bringing into existence the universe and on account of which It got the nomenclature as Īśvara and by the instrumentality of which He brought into being step by step, the universe consisting of the three Guṇas. Since this Māyā principle has originated with the power of Īśvara and is subservient to Him, the Īśvara is called the Lord of Yogamāyā.
Īśvara, who is the prime saguṇa (with attributes) form of the Supreme Spirit, and the poet's prime God Nārāyaṇa are one and the same. There is a legend that Prahlāda the celebrated boy-devotee by the dint of his Nāma Bhakti (devout attachment to the God's name) could secure the *darśana* (vision) of Lord Nārāyaṇa.

75. Thy name is akin to Thee in virtue!

O Lord, Thy name is equivalent to Thee in virtues, not an iota less. Not only this, but it has an additional quality too; and that prominent quality is lacking in Thee in that Thy name is within the reach of everyone. Besides, O Jagannāyaka, it neither harasses its singer nor suffers him to degenerate even for a moment (as Thou didst with King Bali—of course ultimately for the good of the world as well as of the person himself).

Tumhāsamaci he guṇe, aṇu uṇe nase nāma, hā —
Dise adhikahī, tasā guṇa tulā asenā mahā;
Sadaiva bhalatyāsahī sulabha, āṇakhi gāyakā —
Chaḷī na, na adhogati kṣaṇahi de, jagannāyakā!

76. King Bali as also the whole earth was sanctified by Thy foot!

O Lord, even though King Bali was persecuted (by Thee), yet he could not be vanquished altogether as he was really mighty. He is respected not only by me but by all. (There is however, nothing to be astonished at this. Even gold (which is inanimate and dull) sustains all sorts of hard tests to which it is subjected by the valuer (and it stands the test). It is, therefore, quite obvious that Bali (being animate and intelligent) could sustain all sorts of harassment and stand Thy test! Besides, (by the touch of Thy foot which persecuted Bali) not only Bali, the son of Virocana, but also the entire earth was sanctified.[1]

Chaḷī nṛpa Baḷī baḷi tarica to nase āṭalā;
Game bahu bhalā, malā na sakalāsahi vātalā;
Parikṣaka karī, tase jaḍahi sośite hemahī;
Na kevaḷa Virocanātmaja tare pade, he mahī.

1. Refer *Bhāgavata*, VIII cantos 18 to 23.

77. Bali attained greatness because of his persecution by Thee!

O Lord, how could Bali have earned such a conspicuous fame which is esteemed by the wise hadst Thou not thus tormented him? Similarly, how could the river Gaṅgā (the destroyer of all sins) have originated from Thy feet?[1] And how could that lustrous wreath of pearls of the sparkling flow of the Gaṅgā have added to the beauty of this Triloki-Sundari? (In short, it would be more appropriate to say that what Thou hast done to Bali was not his persecution but in fact a boon conferred on him![2])

Asā na karitā jarī chaḷa, tarī Prabho, to bhalī —
Sukīrti kaśī pāvatā; kavisabhā jiṇe śobhalī?
Padī upajatī nadī kaśī, kaśī trilokī satī
Aśā atula mauktikāvaliviṇe barī dīsatī?

1. Vāmana is the fifth incarnation of God Viṣṇu. The legend goes that when He started to measure the universe with His foot, He covered the entire earth with one foot. When He lifted the other one, the frying-pan of the universe was broken with the jolt of His toe and the current of the Gaṅgā, River of the Heaven, thereby descended on the earth.
2. When the King Bali was performing the sacrifice, Lord Viṣṇu disguising Himself as a Brahmin lad (who had undergone investiture with sacrificial thread) approached him and obtained from him a solemn promise of the gift of a three-pace space. Viṣṇu instantly assuming an infinitely stupendous form filled the entire earth with his first step and covered the whole universe with the second one! There being no space left for the third step He placed it on Bali's head at his request and pressed him down into the Pātāla (the lower world)! Viṣṇu resorted to all this harassment of Bali to test if he could keep his word. On being convinced that he stood the test, Viṣṇu bestowed on him the Kingdom of Pātāla and remained permanently as his Dvārapāla. As Bali remained steadfast in his word of honour, he earned an everlasting fame throughout the world and the earth too was benefited with the current of the sacred Gaṅgā's water that it received.

78. I am not strong enough to sustain Thy harassment

But O Lord, I do not want to be similarly harassed since I do not have that much sturdiness to endure it. I would not at all mind even if I do not get a fame like Bali. O Lord, those unique chowries befit only a king like Bali. It would be simply futile and a mockery if they were to be availed of by a trifling person like me. I would rather prefer to remain without fame. How didst even Thou take all that fascination for the rough rustic garments when Thou hadst been in Gokula? O Lord, how dost Thou not understand that a man who is powerful would never accept his defeat willingly?

Nako chaḷa, adhīra mī, taśi na kīrti ho; cāmare
Nṛpāsi ucite; vṛthā, miravilī jarī pāmare;
Akīrtica aso, ruce tuja kaśī vrajī kāṁbaḷī?
Ase na samajā kase, varila hārilā kā baḷī?

79. But why wouldst Thou harass me at all!

But O the compassionate Lord, why wouldst Thou at all harass this weakling! The warriors kill warriors in a battle but never terrify the cowards. Therefore, whatever little favour Thou wilt do to me will be more than enough! O Lord, who art the protector of those who come to Thee for refuge, even though I have come to Thee for shelter having been lost in the darkness[1] of the woods,[2] yet I am enduring lot of hardship! (Just as this situation is not congenial to my interests, it equally does little credit to Thy vow as the saviour of those who come to Thee for shelter!)

Chaḷāla kṛpaṇāsi kā? aji! dayānidhe! kāpitī
Bhaṭāsi bhaṭa saṅgarī pari na kātarā dāpitī;
Karāla titakī kṛpā bahu; aho śaraṇyā, tamī —
Buḍoni śaraṇāgata śramatase araṇyāta mī.

1. Ignorance and sorrows.
2. Worldly life.

80. Thy feet protected the sages performing austerities.

O Lord Nārāyaṇa, the moment the words 'hardship' and 'woods'[1] came to my mouth, I have been reminded of Thy (incarnation as Rāma) bewitching feet. For O the Lord of Sītā! Thy very feet made their way hastily towards the forest (Daṇḍakāraṇya) for the protection (from the demons) of the Brahmins engaged in austerities as if it was the fruit of their penance!

Mukhāsi java pātalī 'śrama, araṇya' aiśī pade
Nijasmṛtisa jāhalī viṣaya tī tava śrīpade;
Gurūktisa karāvayā saphala, jānakījīvanā,
Dharāsuratapaphaḷe tvarita dhāvalī ji vanā.

1. Which have appeared in the previous verse.

81. Thou hadst been very kind in Thy Rāmāvatāra.

O Lord, in the period of Thy incarnation as Rāma, Thou hadst been truly very kind. How then hast Thou become so hard-hearted now? Let Thy mind ponder over this just for a while. That time stricken with the grief of Sītā's separation, Thou hadst roamed lamenting throughout the forest crying out 'Oh my Sītā, Oh my beloved Sītā' like a crazy man. (How then hast Thou become devoid of love now?) O God, I admit I lack the quality of speaking gently.[1] O Lord, I do certainly deserve Thy compassion!

Tayī prabhuvarā! tase sadaya, kā ase āja ho?
Vicāruni pahā bare nijamanī, mahārāja ho!
Vanovani phirā piśāpari, mhaṇā, ahorātra 'hā'!
Nase kuśala bhāṣaṇī, pari ase kṛpāpātra hā.

1. Since I have addressed Thee as 'crazy'.

82. Ignoring great sages Thou befriended the monkeys!

O Lord, Thou hadst made friendship with the monkeys leaving aside the great sages who like the burning of wood in a fire, had undergone strictest austerities to have your company. Dost Thou consider mine speech more inelegant than Sītā's for whose sake Thou hadst to do such odd things and also to invite lot of calamities?

Samāgama tujhā ghado mhaṇuni jāhale lākaḍe,
Taponali tase muni tyajuni jodilī mākaḍe;
Ayukta bahu jyā janāstava ghaḍe, paḍe sākaḍe,
Taduktihuni āmuce bahuta bolaṇe vākaḍe!

83. Why didst Thou obey Sītā's unwise demand?

O Lord, Thou who captivatest the minds of the three worlds and art the ocean of power and of other virtues was insisted by Sītā, Thy dear wife, to bring for her the golden deer by all means and thus asked Thee to do an ignoble act!

(But why after all didst Thou obey it?) Henpecked husbands openly gulp the dictates of their wives willingly rejecting the nectar! (an experience of which everybody is aware).

Jagattrayamanoharā, balaguṇaikaratnākarā,
Mhaṇe 'kanakaraṅku dyā maja, mahā prayatnā karā'
Priyāhi aśi jāhalī tuja kukārya ājñāpitī;
Sudhā tyajuni kāmuka pragaṭa aṅganājñā pitī.

84. Sītā failed to appreciate Lakṣmaṇa's sincere services

Even though Lakṣmaṇa used to discharge his duties promptly like a faithful attendant, yet Sītā never expressed in return any regard for him! He never failed in his duties, yet she did not have even a word of appreciation for his toil. On the contrary she had reprimanded him. Kindly enquire from Sītā herself whether what I say is true or otherwise without in any way feeling offended. As I happen to be poor and humble, O Lord, kindly dost not go on thrashing me like cotton for nothing!

Svadāsa samayī jape tari na de varā, cākarī —
Cuke na pari sārthaka śrama na devarācā karī;
Vadehi bhalateci, te tisaci, kopa ṭākā, pusā;
Ase mṛdu mhaṇoni bā, maja na dhopaṭā kāpusā.

85. We find fault with what we dislike!

Whatever is not to our liking appears defective to our eyes. Similarly that which suits to our taste seems pleasing even though faulty! A child even when it gets dirty while crawling in mud does give pleasure to its parents. (Why to quote remote instances?) Kindly try to recollect Thy own childhood. In Thy childhood (in Thy incarnation as Kṛṣṇa) was mother Yaśodā not holding Thee caressingly to her bosom even though due to the dust in which Thou played, Thy clothes had become dirty?

Na je priya, sadoṣa te; priya sadoṣahi cāṅgale;
Svatoka pitarā ruce, jarihi kardamī rāṅgale;
Tulāci dhari poṭiśī kaśi tadā yaśodā bare?
Jarī maḷaviśī rajomalinakāya tū aṁbare.

86. Thy pranks were more pleasing to Yaśodā than Thy praise!

The Gopis used to make so many complaints with Yaśodā (about Thy pranks). But she used to derive more pleasure from these complaints than even from the praise they showered on Thee for Thy virtues! Once however, she did not excuse Thee; yet Thou did not fail to indulge in lots of pranks. But though she wanted to strike terror in Thy mind she eventually refrained from doing so. On the contrary (observing Thy horrified and pale face) she not only gave up her resolve to give Thee a beating but also untied Thy hands which she had bound! (Refer *Bhāgavata*, X-9)

Tujhe kathiti gopikā vividha tīsa bobhāṭa, te —
Sukhaprada guṇastavāparisa jāhale vāṭate;
Kṣamā na karī ekadā, tarihi phāra khoḍī karā
Na deci bhaya, tāḍanodyamasameta soḍī karā.

87. Yaśodā had not bothered Thee as much as Thou didst her.

Thou mayest perhaps say that mother Yaśodā (even though she had not castigated me) did after all tie my hands! But O Lord, kindly remember that she did not bother Thee, at least not to the extent to which Thou hadst done her. When she took a rope to bind Thee, why should she have been obliged to take another one to supplement it if the first one was adequate? O God, Gopī Yaśodā was certainly not able to bind Thee but it was purely Thy mercy which caused Thee to be bound! (On noticing the futile labour Thy mother was putting in to bind Thee, Thou took pity on her and allowed Thyself to be bound!) (Refer *Ibid.*)

Jarī mhaṇasi 'bāndhile'tari na kaṣṭavīle; karā —
Vicāra; jaśi kaṣṭavā, taśi na kaṣṭavī lekarā;
Yatheṣṭa purate jarī prathama dāma kā sāṅdhitī?
Na tī prabala gopikā; tuja tujhī dayā bāndhitī.

88. Have the devotees forfeited Thy mercy?

O Lord, Thou too hadst overawed the King Bali likewise. Should it, therefore, be concluded that the natural compassion of Thy heart which is to us as our mother, had been abruptly swept out by Thee? Sire, the elders are enraged (with children) but their anger is only short-lived. Though water becomes hot for a while due to the proximity of fire, it does not forsake its natural coolness for ever![1]

> Tumhīhi baḷi bāndhilā, mhaṇuni āmucī māya jī —
> Manāta sahajā dayā, nipaṭa ṭākilī kāya? jī
> Sakopa disatī guru kṣaṇabharīca je tāpale
> jala jvalana saṅgame, tyaji na śaitya te āpale.

1. Refer *Bhāgavata*, VIII, cantos 18 to 23.

89. How can a father be cruel to his erring child?

O Lord, Thy feet enjoy a high renown for being 'most kind'. How then can they become callous even for a moment for the faults of the ignorant and the weak? A father is never cruel. He says to himself that his sons should not turn out to be block-heads. Sire, which patient would ever like to take bitter medicines willingly who is accustomed to unwholesome diet? (He has to be administered the medicines forcibly. In the same way intractable boys have to be rectified through punishment only!)

Prasiddha tumace mahāsadaya pāya; jīvākaḍe —
Cukī, mhaṇuni hotila kṣaṇahi kāya, jī! vākaḍe?
Na niṣṭhura pitā; mhaṇe mani, 'na ho prajā ṭoṇapī'
Apathyaruci rugṇa to kaṭuka okhade koṇa pī?

90. Thou emancipated even the wicked whom Thou killed!

O Lord, the number of the wicked whom Thou hast killed in battles is countless. However, Thou hast not cruelly put them to death but hast in fact uplifted them by Thy grace! O God, Thou art the father of this world and all the creatures are Thy progeny. Thou dost get enraged with them but even after expressing Thy wrath, Thou dost not fail to give them a piece of candy![1] One who is out to harm others does not give them nectar (but only poison); But Thou conferest the nectar of emancipation even on the villainous.

Asaṅkhya khala saṅgarī nijakarī tuvā mārile;
Na niṣṭhurapaṇe, kṛpā karuni te bhavī tārile;
Jagajjanaka tū, mule sakala jīva, yā bhātuke —
Daṭāvunihi deśi bā; amṛta nedije ghātuke.

1. Liberation.

91. Thou liberated Pūtanā who administered poison to Thee!

O Lord, just as a female crane pretending to be calm and quiet grabs and gulps a fish, in the same way the sinful and villainous Pūtanā[1] was designing to kill Thee. However, to Pūtanā who made Thee suck poison (applied to her breast), Thou gavest in return the nectar of liberation! The righteous do understand this magnanimity of Thine even though the wicked may like to overlook it.

Varī prakaṭa śāṅtilā dhari, parantu mīnā bakī —
Giḷī; taśi tulā ṭape sukṛtabuddhihīnā bakī,
Jiṇe garala pājile amṛta pājile tīsa te
Khalāsi na diso bhalepaṇa, khare bhalyā dīsate.

1. In order to kill Śrī Kṛṣṇa, she got him to suck milk from her breast to which poison was applied by her.

92. Thou never neglectest Thy devotees even if guilty.

O Lord, we do not pay any heed to good advice and indulge in pernicious deeds and would continue to do so in future also. (We are thus childish and stupid.) But Thou who art our gracious and loving father exclaimest thus— 'What am I to do? The child doesn't heed!' But O Lord, just as Nanda, the king of the cowherds never used to be displeased with Thee, in the same way Thy devotees never suffer any negligence at Thy hands!

Sadāhi hita nāyako, bahu apāya kele karū
Tarī sakṛpa bāpa tū mhaṇasi, 'nāyake lekarū';
Kadhī na karisī, Prabho, bhajakabāḷakopekṣaṇa
Na tūjavari jyāparī paśupapāḷa kope kṣaṇa.

93. Thou art our true father!

O Lord, Thou art alone our true father, for who is the other God that has created all these beings? (of course, none else). It is Thy lotus-like foot which not only gives of its own accord the desired beneficial things to this world but also causes them to be given.[1] O Hari, let Thy favour continue to remain unending. May we never incur Thy wrath who art our father, for who else would look after a sinner like me?[2]

Kharā janaka tū, janā itara koṇa ho deva vī?
Samīhita phaḷe jagā tava padābja de, devavī;
Asīca karuṇā aso Hari, kadhī na bhaṅgo pitā;
Āśā maja asādhulā itara koṇa saṅgopitā?

1. Through various deities, saints, sacred places etc.
2. Compare 'Your heavenly Father knoweth that you have need of all these things'. New Testament, St. Matthew, vi-32.

94. Thou dost not discard even a wretch!

(It is generally noticed that) A son who is learned, earns his livelihood, obedient and is a good householder owning the responsibilities of maintaining the family, wins the affection of his father. But if a son does not answer this description, the father does not tolerate that worthless fellow even for a moment![1] But O God, Thou dost like even such a wretch and dost not fail to look after him!

Suvidya, dhana meḷavī, vacana āyake, āvarī
Prapañca, bhara ghe śirī, kari kṛpā pitā tyāvarī;
Asā jari nase, ruce tari na to abhadra kṣaṇa;
Tasā tujaci āvaḍe; karisi tūci tadrakṣaṇa.

1. Compare 'The fundamental defect of fathers is that they want their children to be a credit to them'. — Bertrand Russell

95. A mother's debt can never be repaid.

O God, if a father is disgusted with a worthless son, let him do so, but a mother is never sick and tired of him. A mother whose heart is always full of the nectar of mercy never gets turbid (by anger or despise) even on account of such a wretched son who is like a black collyrium on the renown of the family! The cover of mercy of the other preceptors no doubt protects (the child or the disciple), yet it does fall short of its requirement. (A mother's protective cover however fully shields the child. The virtuous, therefore, say that a mother's debt can never be repaid!

Pitā jari viṭe, viṭo; na jananī kuputrī viṭe;
Dayāmṛtarasārdradhī na kulakajjale tyā kiṭe;
Prasādapaṭa jhākitī, pari parā gurūnce thiṭe
Mhaṇūni mhaṇati bhale 'na ṛṇa janmadece phiṭe'.

96. Thy compassion forsakest not the sinful wretch!

O God, unfortunately because of hundreds of reasons planned by destiny even a mother may sometimes get weary of her son. Just as in this evil Kaliyuga a study of the sacred Vedas has lost its lustre having fallen in the hands of the undeserving; even so, a mother's pure love may get contaminated. But O Lord, just as the river Gaṅgā which has originated from Thy foot does not retract from her mission of washing away the sins of the world, similarly Thy compassion too never gets weary of the sinful wretch!

Viṭela jananīhi kī śata racī nimitte vidhī;
Maḷe kaliyugī śṛtī jaśi khaḷī, ticī tevi dhī
Kadācita viṭela; bā, tava dayā na dīnāvarī;
Jaśī jagadaghakṣayī kara bhavannadī nāvarī.

97. Thy mercy is the real mother!

O God, Thy grace is the real mother and all the beings are her offsprings. And these (whom we call as mothers) who are in fact nurses trained in the teachings of Thy 'Grace' shower their kindness on us.[1] Even if this secret is known, it is not that the virtuous men of wisdom relinquish their reverence for their parents. O Lord, Thou too used to give a great reverence to thy mother-like milkmaid, Yaśodā. So (even though our mothers of whom we are born fall in the category of our nurses when compared to Thy Grace) what is wrong if the common men address their Janmadātrī as 'mother'?

Kṛpāci jananī tujhī, sakala jīva dāyāda; yā —
Tiṇeci upadeśilyā kariti sarva dāyā dāyā;
Ase umajatā bhale na gurubhāva to ṭākitī;
Matā tujasi gopikā, maga janāsa toṭā kitī?

1. A mother's love is a fraction of the God's grace. The impulse of a mother's love for her child has its origin in the Divine compassion.

98. Thou hadst conferred beatitude both on Devakī and Pūtanā

O Lord, alike Thy mother Devakī on whom Thou bestowed (final liberation and) supreme bliss, Thou also liberated the female demon Pūtanā who having filled poison in the pitcher of her breast made Thee to suck it. Then how could those cows and Nanda's wife Yaśodā[1] (who were not pernicious like Pūtanā but were very affectionate and had reared Thee on their milk) fail to attain the status of motherhood? The happiness which Thou showered on them is limitless. Who would not like to sing such stories of Thy grand saga?

Bharoni kucakumbha jī viṣarase mukhī de bakī,
Prabho tisahi ṭheviśī jaśi mahāsukhī Devakī;
Na hoti jananī kaśā paśupadāra, gāī? layā
Na pāvatica tatsukhe, kṛti na koṇa gāila yā?

1. Yaśodā, the wife of Nanda had brought up Kṛṣṇa in Vṛandāvana since his birth as her own son.

99. Thou alone hast boundless compassion

O Hari, Thou alone hast such[1] compassion. O God, even after bestowing Thy beneficent and mountain-like favour, Thou who art dear to me as my very breath, treatest it as insignificant as an atom! The marriageable daughter in the form of the poetry by eminent poets, is simply fascinated by this virtue which is Thy priceless ornament. Would anyone then ever like to say that Thy oft-sung glories may not be sung time and again?

Aśī tari kṛtajñatā, Hari, tujhyāca ṭhayī agā!
Sakhyā, aṇuci māniśī, karuni suprasādā agā;
Bhule sukavivāgvadhū tava guṇā anarghyā nagā
Mhaṇela jana koṇa, kī 'yaśa punaḥ-punhā te na gā'?

1. Endless and non-retracting.

100. Who would not like to sing Thy saga again and again?

O Lord, Thou art omniscient. Kindly, therefore, answer the following queries to my complete satisfaction. How could a person be called a connoisseur who would feel bored and say 'Oh! the same old story is again being repeated'. O Lord, the saga of Thy glory in which even an ascetic like Śuka (who was selfless and unattached) had experienced novelty of joy at every moment, would never fail to fascinate one and all except those who are uninterested, emotionless and unfortunate persons!

Tumhī bahu bhale, malā umaja hoya aise kathā;
Kasā rasika to? 'punhā' jari mhaṇela 'ālī kathā';
Pratikṣaṇa navīca de ruci, Śukāhi saṁnyāsiyā;
Na mohiti bhavatkathā arasikā adhanyāsi yā!

101. Only the connoisseurs are overwhelmed by Thy saga

Even though the self-same story may mount again and again on the pedestal of the ear, yet it is only the genuine connoisseurs who get immersed in the emotional fervour stirred up by it. Others, namely those uninterested, however, feel bored. A coquettish woman by making eyes at the gay captures their hearts. But even if she actually kisses an effeminate fellow it produces on him no effect whatsoever!

Kathā śravaṇacatvarī jari punaḥpunhā ye, rate,
Mahārasika tadrasī, viṭati aikatā yera te;
Vilokuni vilāsinījana punaḥpunhā kāmukā
Kari vaśa; navhe bulā vivaśa, gheinā kā mukā!

102. The devotee feels lonely if he fails to hear Thy saga

O Lord, just as Rādhā who was dearer to Thee than Thy body had enchanted Thee, even so, Thy saga allures Thy devotee. O Lord, just as Thou in spite of being the spouse of Lakṣmī, feelest Thy home as a forest in the absence of Rādhā's company in the same way a devotee feels himself to be in wilderness! (if he fails to hear Thy saga).

Kathā supuruṣā tujhī vaśa taśī karī, Rādhikā,
Jaśī tuja, jilā svaye mhaṇasi tū 'śarīrādhikā';
Tice na ghaḍatā, ramāhṛdayavallabhā, sevana
Prabho, tuja jase, tase matisa geha bhāse vana.

103. Thy saga is more bewitching than Mohinī!

O Lord, Thy saga is enchanting to the world. Even Thy appearance in the guise of Mohinī[1] was not so bewitching. Thy Mohinī form may have lured the demons, but this saga has enthralled many a self-restrained hermit! This is not to say that Mohinī had never captivated any recluse, but even though Mohinī had enchanted Śaṅkara, the destroyer of Dakṣa,[2] how could (the wife-mad) Śaṅkara who has given a seat to His beloved spouse Gaṅgā on his head, be regarded as a devout observer of the vows enjoined on a hermit? (He cannot truly be called a hermit!)

Kathā bhuvanamohinī aśī na Mohinī hoya; tī
Haro asuradhī; hiṇe bhulavile kitī ho yatī?
Navhe na mhaṇave; aso; jari vimohilā dakṣahā,
Priyā basavilī śirī munipathī kasā dakṣa hā?

---

1. After 'Samudramanthana' (churning of the sea), the demons started quarreling for the Amṛta (nectar). With a view, therefore, to hoodwink them (by giving them wine instead of the nectar) Lord Viṣṇu assumed the form of Mohinī. She was so exquisitely charming that even God Śaṅkara the Lord of ascetics, became infatuated with her! No wonder then that Mohinī could delude the demons by keeping them engrossed in drinking wine! (*Bhāgavata*, VIII-12)
2. Once Dakṣa performed a yajña (sacrifice) but did not invite his daughter Pārvatī or Śaṅkara the son-in-law on the occasion. Pārvatī although uninvited, however attended it contrary to Śaṅkara's wishes. On being insulted there, she threw herself into the sacrificial fire. Śaṅkara reached the scene shortly when Vīrabhadra, who originated from his matted hair destroyed the yajña and also killed Dakṣa. (*Ibid.*, IV 2 to 5)

104. Unlike Thy saga, Mohinī was discriminative

O God, alike Mohinī the saga of Thy glory also enchants the Gods, demons, human beings, Nāgas and others; yet after having allured them does not discard them or make any discrimination[1] between them, but gives them real nectar.[2] Mohinī pretended to give nectar to the demons whom she had captivated but then the same relentless Mohinī killed them all while they were about to drink the nectar![3]

Surāsuranaroragā bhulavunī kathā na tyajī;
Na bheda kari paṅkticā; amṛta pājitī satya jī;
Tiṇe jari sudhārasa svaratamānasā pājilā,
Vadhī amṛta ghoṭitā, drava na yeci bāpā! jilā.

1. Giving of nectar to the gods and wine to the demons.
2. Final emancipation.
3. In order to delude the demons who were clamouring for the nectar, Mohinī began to serve them wine instead, pretending that it was the nectar and was passing the real nectar on to the gods. Two of the demons, viz., Rāhū and Ketū who came to know the fraud practised upon them disguising themselves as gods joined the group in which nectar was being served by Mohinī. But very soon the identity of these demons who were disguised as gods, came to light and they were instantly executed before the nectar could pass down their throats! (*Bhāgavata*, VIII-9)

105. Thy saga though bewitching confers liberation!

O Lord, those who have faith in Thy saga stand to be benefited. But Mohinī is well known to the world as one who had deceived the demons. How could then Thy saga fall in her category? Thy saga does similarly enchant but it bestows on the enchanted, the nectar of final liberation by cutting asunder the bonds of the deeds of his previous births! It amply proves that it is kind even in its deception!

Abhīṣṭa varitāta, je tava kathesa viśvāsatī;
Bhalī asuravañcanī śṛta aseci viśvāsa tī;
Kathā kaśi sakhī ticī? ṭhakavunī harī sañcite
Tarī amṛta de; ase sadaya, dākhavī vañcite.

106. A mother deluding her child for its good, cannot be said to be cruel

O Lord, I beseech Thee to listen to what I say. I would not then at all mind even if the people who do not understand the essence of the matter, laugh at me. Could a mother be taken as guilty of callousness if on finding her beloved child about to swallow 'Somala', takes it away deceitfully from his hand and replaces it by lot of sugar?

Karā śravaṇa yevaḍhe apaṭu loka hāso malā;
Aho, jari giḷāvayā priyakumāra ghe somalā,
Tayāsi ṭhakavūni, de bahuta śarkarā māya jī,
Tilā svaśiśuvañcane adayatā śive kāya, jī?

107. Am I not both Mohinī and saga?—Lord Nārāyaṇa

Therefore, O Lord, Thy saga which fulfils the desires of Thy humble servants is doubtless far superior to Mohinī. Thou mayest say 'I am myself both Mohinī and saga. How can there be any difference between them? Just as people equally obtain emancipation by bathing in the current of the white Gaṅgā and the blackish Yamunā, similarly they are liberated alike by Mohinī and the saga.'

Mhaṇoni bahu Mohinīhuni bhalī kathā he tuji
Abhiṣṭa phala dyāvayā natamanorathā hetu ji;
Mhaṇāla jari, mīca tyā, viṣama kāya doghīta re?
Jasā jana sitā sitābhidhanadīsadoghī tare

108-9. Thy saga is purer than Mohini.

O Lord, The saga of Thy glory is certainly purer than Thy figure in Mohinī's disguise. The Gaṅgā and the Yamunā are not at all different and realising their oneness all the wise pay obeisance to them. However, I am telling Thee the experience of the common folk. But in narrating it I wish, I may not incur even the slightest sin!

Ahā! bahu viśuddha he, Prabhu! tava svarūpāhunī;
Na bhinnatanu tyā; bhale bhajati, ekatā pāhunī;
Parantu vadato janānubhava, nātaḷo pāpa, gā!
Taśī na Yamunā game, jaśī game nilimpāpagā.

The Yamunā is not held in such high esteem by the common men as the divine Gaṅgā who abides on the very head of God Śaṅkara, the preceptor of the universe. Even the mud of her waters ranks higher in sanctity than the transparent brightness of the Autumn moon; besides, many a man who died in her waters attained union with God Viṣṇu or God Śiva![1] Those who are wise would even under duress, never declare molasses to be equal to the nectar!

Jagadgurumaheśvaraprabhuśirī jice nāndaṇe,
Jicyā jaḷamaḷe tuḷe na śardinduce cāndaṇe,
Prajā Hariharāaśā yadudarī anekā, kavī
Bhiūni mhaṇatīla kā? 'jaśī sudhā, taśī 'Kākavī.'

1. It is believed that a person who happens to die in the current of the Gaṅgā attains intimate union either with God Viṣṇu on God Śiva according to the deity of which he is a devotee!

110. Mohinī is Yamunā while Thy saga is Gaṅgā!

O Nārāyaṇa, who art of a dark-blue lotus-like complexion, if Thou sayest that Thy figure in the guise of Mohinī could be compared to Yamunā, I shall view the comparison as fully justified. Then I too shall compare the saga of Thy greatness which is as pure as a white lily sprouting forth in a sea of the nectar to the divine river Gaṅgā!

Tulīna Yamunesave, kuvalayadyutiśyāmalā!
Mhaṇāla jari mohinī nijatanū, avaśyā malā;
Tulīna amṛtodadhiprabhavapuṇḍarīkāmalā;
Kathā suradhunīsave, sujana jīta viśrāmalā.

111. Thy saga is doubtless exquisite

O Lord, one who has heard the entire *Bhāgavata Purāṇa* from a well known orator will testify to the fact that the saga of Thy glory is undoubtedly superb. Kindly dost not consider him as uncompromising for it is not I alone who think that this *Bhāgavata Kathā* is unique and decked with the glories of Gods but those elders who have wider learning than I also feel likewise. Why go far away? Better consult Thy scholarly preceptor Sāndīpani,[1] the bestower of boons on Thee!

> Śukodita purāṇa jyā śravaṇa sanmukhe sāgrahī
> Mhaṇela 'atulā kathā'; jhaṇi mhaṇāla, 'to āgrahī'
> Na kevaḷa malāci he nirupamā, yaśomaṇḍitā,
> Gurūsahi game,pusā svavaradā mahāpaṇḍitā.

1. Sage Sāndipani was Kṛṣṇa's preceptor. Sudāmā was Kṛṣṇa's fellow-student and both were staying with Sāndipani. Since then they became intimate friends.

112. Thy saga enchants even Thee!

O Lord, though Mohinī had enticed all, yet she had not enticed Thee! Further, she had ultimately forsaken those whom she had allured. But this saga of Thy glory is altogether a different tale. It keeps even Thee under its spell! Thou mayest kindly recollect Thy own experience. As narrated by Thee to Nārada, Thy saga by its impelling power keeps Thee spellbound, just as a specially powerful medicine, when mixed with the unstable mercury, makes the latter stable and solid!

Prabho, tuja na Mohinī bhulavi; mohilā tohi tī
Tyajī jana; navhe taśī, tuja tujhī kathā mohitī;
Nijānubhava tū pahā; jaśī mahauṣadhī pāradā,
Tulā sthira baḷe karī, kaḷavile tuvā Nāradā.

113. I am always there where my saga is sung!

O Lord, Thou Thyself hast told the great sage Nārada *tatra tiṣthāmi,*[1] i.e. 'I reside' (where the saga of My greatness is being sung by My devotees). On the strength of this admission of Thine own, I assert that Thou dost long to hear Thy saga being sung. O God, just as Thy permanent abode art in Thy saga, even so kindly see that my mind remains firmly adhered to it. O the wish-tree of Thy devotees, let my desire be fulfilled!

> Surarṣijavaḷī svaye vadasi, 'tatra tiṣṭhāmi'; yā —
> Tujhyāci vacane mhaṇe tuja 'Kathāvaśa' svāmiyā!
> Jasā sthira katheta tū sthira karī tase yā manā;
> Svabhaktasurapādapā, saphala he aso kāmanā.

1. The poet quotes here verbatim the sanskrit words *tatra tiṣthāmi* from the famous saying of Lord Kṛṣṇa to Nārada (in the Purāṇas), '*nāhaṁ vasāmi vaikunṭhe yogināṁ hṛdaye ravau/madbhaktā yatra gāyanti tatra tiṣthāmi narada.*'

114. 'May I always sing Thy glory!' says Nārada

Says Nārada, 'O God, may Thy grand saga be always sung by me. Let people say that the other means, viz, practice of yoga etc. of realising Thee are easier to follow.' Nārada does not pay any heed to the numerous means for the attainment of Mokṣa other than the singing of Thy saga. Putting his Brahma Vīṇā into tune, he keeps on dancing in the congregation of the Vaiṣṇavas completely wrapped up in the love of God!

Surarṣi mhaṇato, 'tujhe yaśaci dhanya yo gāyanā —
Malā, kavi mhaṇota te sukhada anyayogāyanā';
Vimuktibahusādhane taditare gaṇīnāca to
Sajūni varavallakī tava sabhāṅgaṇī nācato.

115. Nārada attained status of Brahmadeva's son due to deep devotion.

O Lord, as Nārada had the fortune to hear the saga of Thy glories from Thy devotees, he acquired the unique distinction of becoming Brahmadeva's[1] son in his next birth! Therefore, all the saints always sing his fame. O Lord, who takest Thy devotees safely to the other shore of the sea of this worldly existence, the sage Nārada does not fail to remember at every moment the poor and pitiable condition of his previous birth and the limitless grace that Thou hast bestowed on him!

> Tujhe carita sanmukhe śravaṇa jāhale, yāstava —
> Prajāpatisutatva ye, kariti sādhu jyācā stava;
> Svanīcapaṇa māgile, bahu dayā aśī, Nāradā —
> Smare ghaḍighaḍī, Prabho! bhavapayodhicyā pāradā.

1. In his previous birth Nārada lived a life of abject poverty but in the company of the righteous, he cultivated a passion for singing the praises of God and soon attained the status of a great sage. Ultimately, he became Lord Brahmadeva's 'Mānasaputra' and earned the reputation as the pioneer divine-sage of the cult of devotion throughout the world.

116. Thy glory is the saviour of beings!

O Lord, Thy glory is thus our saviour. But it cannot of its own, accomplish this feat without somebody's help. A sword can kill an enemy only if it gets the assistance of a dexterous swordsman. In the same way, the hearts of the ignorant cannot dive deep into the divine joy obtainable from singing Thy saga until they happen to meet the devotees of God and the righteous provide their company to them.

Tujhe yaśaci tārite, pari na kevaḷā tārave;
Sahāya asilā ase, tarica śatrulā mārave;
Na bhāgavata bheṭatā, na ghaḍatāhi satsaṅgatī,
Na ajñahṛdaye tasī tava yaśorasī raṅgatī.

117. Thy fame aided by saints emancipates the beings

If a boat does not have an able helmsman, it not only sinks in the sea, but causes its crew and passengers to be sunk also. It cannot of its own accord reach the shore. Even so, O Lord, Thy fame can take the beings quickly to the other shore of the sea of this worldly life only when it is assisted by Thy devout followers.

Buḍe, buḍavi sāgarī tari, sukarṇadhārāvinā,
Sahāya nasatā svaye paratatāsi tī dāvinā;
Sahāya bhagavajjanā tava sukīrti jevhā karī,
Tayīca utarī bhavodadhitaṭī janā laukarī.

118. May I always get the company of the righteous!

(And so, O Lord, my only prayer to Thee is)
May I always get the company of the righteous and may my ears hear the talk of the virtuous only;
May my mind be divested of its evil aptitudes and abhor worldly pleasures;
May my mind take refuge at the lotus-like pure and tender feet of the saints and stick to its place intractably even if discarded by them;
And even in spite of this, if it does suffer separation from the feet of the saints, it should weep profusely; yet it should get itself lost in Thy sacred saga!

Susaṅgati sadā ghaḍo sujanavākya kānī paḍo,
Kalaṅka maticā jhaḍo, viṣaya sarvathā nāvaḍo;
Sadaṅdhrikamaḷī daḍo, muraḍitā haṭāne aḍo;
Viyoga ghaḍatā raḍo mana bhavaccaritrī jaḍo!

119. May my mind never become unstable!

O Lord, may my resolve never shake and may the nuisance of the impediments put up by the wicked disappear;
May my mind remain steadfast in Thy worship and tread upon the path shown by the saints;
May my heart be illumined by self-knowledge and may my self-concept wither away.
My mind which after being cleansed has set forth following the path of devotion, may never again get itself contaminated with sensual desires and may all my sins be reduced to ashes by self-realisation.

Na niścaya kadhī ḍhaḷo, kujanavighnabādhā ṭaḷo;
Na citta bhajanī caḷo, mati saduktamārgī vaḷo,
Svatatva hṛdayā kaḷo, durabhimāna sārā gaḷo,
Punhā na mana he maḷo, durita ātmabodhe jaḷo.

120. May the rosary of Thy names be always on my tongue!

O God, mayest Thy Nāmāvalī which is the abode of all that is auspicious, which is very kind and fulfils all our desires instantaneously, always remain on my tongue. It is obvious that just as Thou, who fillest the three worlds, bestowest Thy compassion on Thy humble servants, even so Thy Nāmāvalī too, does always protect them!

Mukhī Hari vaso tujhī kuśaladhāmanāmāvalī,
Kṣaṇāta puravīla jī sakala kāmanā māvalī;
Kṛpā karisi tū jagattrayanivāsa dāsāvarī,
Taśī prakaṭa he nijāśritajanā sadā sāvarī.

121. O Hari, the cloud of mercy, turn towards this Mayūra!

O Hari, who art the cloud of the nectar of compassion, kindly turn towards this peacock (towards Moropanta the poet) with an intent to do him a favour. Touched by the crying of her babe, a mother takes it up on her hip with profound affection. O God whose feet have been eulogized by the righteous, where canst Thou find such an earnest seeker? Howsoever Thy humble servants might have become heavily laden with sin, it is not at all difficult for Thee to lift them up out of the sea of this worldly life and carry them safe to the other shore!

Dayāmṛta ghanā aho Hari, vaḷā Mayūrākaḍe;
Raḍe śiśu, tayāsi ghe kaḷavaḷoni mātā kaḍe
Asā atithi, dhārmikastutapadā! kadā sāpaḍe?
Tumhā jaḍa bhavārṇavī utaritā na dāsā paḍe.

EPILOGUE

God Rāma who is a cloud of compassion, is a close friend of this frenziedly dancing peacock. He is a tutor (in the dramatic art) and also a vigilant protector of this wild peacock (rustic poet Moropanta) from the threefold tribulations of the woods of this mundane existence. In His true remembrance alone lies the real well-being of this peacock. How can then the poet fail to remember Him? And having remembered Him thus has in his one hundred and twenty one Kekās implored Him for His mercy and favour.[1]

Upasaṁhāra

Kāruṇyām bhoda Rāma priyasakha, guruhī, jo mayūrā naṭācā,
Hotā tāpatrayārta, tvarita bhavavanī rakṣitā rānaṭācā.
Tyāce sāce svabhadra smaraṇa, maga na te tyā kase ye kavīsa?
Kekā, ekā sakhyāte smaruni, kari aśā yekaśe yekavīsa.

1. The poet says that he cherishes the deepest devotion for Lord Rāma akin to the attachment a peacock has for a cloud. A mere remembrance of His name sends a thrill of joy within him and he begins to sing in His honour songs as best as he can, beseeching Him to shower His Grace on him just as at the sight of the dark clouds the joy of the peacock knows no bounds and it begins to dance frenziedly giving out a series of loud screams with the expectation that the clouds would favour it with a soothing shower! In short, Lord Rāma is to the poet what a cloud is to a peacock!

GLOSSARY

Abhaṅga : A particular form of poetic composition. The popular metre used by many of the poet-saints in Marathi language.

Āryā : A kind of metre; a stanza in this metre.

Āptakāma : One whose desires have been gratified.

Agha : The name of a demon.

Ahalyā : The wife of the sage Gautama.

Ajāmiḷa : Was a brahmin but being dissolute earned a disrepute.

Arjuna : One of the five Pāṇḍavas and to whom the Gītā discourse was delivered by Lord Kṛṣṇa on the battle-field of Kurukshetra.

Ayodhyā : The capital of Rāma's kingdom.

Bakī (or Pūtanā) : Name of a female demon.

Bali : Name of a demon king.

Bhāgavata Kathā : A legend from *Bhāgavata Purāṇa*.

Bhāgavata Purāṇa : A popular Hindu mythological work.

Bhasmāsura : The name of a demon.

Bibhiṣaṇa : King Rāvaṇa's brother; was righteous and joined Rāma's camp.

Bhṛgu : Name of a sage.

Brahmadeva : The first deity in the Hindu triad, regarded as the creator of the universe, the other two being Viṣṇu and Maheśa. Viṣṇu is the sustainer and Maheśa the destroyer of the universe.

Brahmaviṇā : The lute of the sage Nārada.

Cātaka : A bird which is supposed to live only on rain-drops.

Dakṣa : Father of Pārvatī in her former birth.

Daṇḍakāraṇya	: Name of the forest in which Lord Rāma stayed for some time with brother Lakṣmaṇa and wife Sītā during the period of exile.
Devakī	: Lord Kṛṣṇa's mother.
Dharmarāja	: The eldest among Pāṇḍavas.
Dhruva	: Name of a celebrated boy-devotee.
Draupadī	: Wife of the Pāṇḍavas.
Dvārapāla	: Door-keeper
Ekanātha	: Famous poet-saint of Maharashtra. Author of *Bhāvārtha Rāmāyaṇa*. Is also famous for his commentary on the eleventh 'Skandha' of *Śrīmadbhāgavata*.
Gokula	: Name of the place where Lord Kṛṣṇa was brought up.
Gajendra	: Name of a legendary elephant.
Gaṅgā	: The most sacred river in India and the female deity presiding over it.
Gopi	: Cowherd's wife.
Govardhana	: Name of a hill.
Guṇatraya	: Three properties of created matter: Satva, Raja and Tama.
Hālāhala	: A deadly poison.
Hari	: Viṣṇu.
Hara	: Śiva.
Indra	: The king of Gods.
Jagannāyaka	: Lord of the universe.

Jāmbavatī	: Daughter of Jāmbuvanta.
Jāmbuvanta	: A monkey born of the yawn of Brahmadeva.
Janmadātrī	: Mother.
Kabīra	: A great Indian poet-saint.
Kailāsa	: Name of a mountain and the residence of Śiva.
Kalī	: Wrangle; Satan.
Kaliyuga	: The fourth or the Iron Age of the world.
Kalpataru	: Wish-yielding tree.
Kāmadhenu	: A cow that fulfils every desire.
Kaṁsa	: King of Mathurā and Kṛṣṇa's maternal uncle.
Kayādhū	: Father of Prahlāda.
Keka	: Peacock's cry.
Kekāvali	: A series of the screams of a peacock.
Khara	: An ass; Name of a demon.
Khari	: A she-ass.
Kṣirasāgara	: Ocean of milk.
Kṛṣṇa	: An incarnation of God Viṣṇu whose life is given in the *Bhāgavata* and *Mahābhārata*.
Kubjā	: The name of a hump-backed female servant at the palace of King Kaṁsa.
Lakṣmaṇa	: Lord Rāma's brother.
Lakṣmī	: Spouse of God Viṣṇu; Goddess of wealth.
Madana	: God of Love.
Mahābhārata	: The famous Hindu epic on the great Bhārata War.

Mandara	: Name of legendary Mountain with which the sea was churned by the Gods and the demons for obtaining the nectar.
Meru	: Name of a mythological mountain.
Mohinī	: Viṣṇu in the form of a fascinating woman.
Mokṣa	: Liberation.
Murāntaka	: God Nārāyaṇa, who killed the demon Mura.
Nāmāvalī	: A roll of names.
Nāmadeva	: Famous poet-saint of Maharashtra, contemporary of Jñāneśvara.
Narasi Mehatā	: Famous poet-saint from Gujarat.
Nirguṇa	: Without attributes.
Nirākāra	: Formless.
Ovī	: A stanza of a particular measure.
Parabrahma	: Supreme spirit.
Parāśara	: Sage Vyāsa's father.
Paramātman	: The Supreme Spirit.
Pātāla	: The lower world.
Patrāvalī	: A plate made of leaves tacked together; designs of creepers and plants.
Paurāṇika	: Mythological, ancient.
Piṅgalā	: Name of a harlot.
Prahlāda	: Name of a celebrated boy-devotee.
Purāṇa	: Hindu mythological works.
Purāntaka	: God Śiva, who killed the demon named Pura.

Rādhā	: Lord Kṛṣṇa's lady-love symbol for deep spiritual love and devotion.
Rādhāramaṇa	: Lover of Rādhā.
Rāma	: Hero of the Rāmāyaṇa epic.
Rāmadāsa	: A great saint from Maharashtra.
Rāvaṇa	: King of Lankā.
Śabarī	: Name of a female 'Bhilla' (forest-dwelling tribe).
Saguṇa	: That has attributes; concrete.
Śaiva	: Devotee of Śiva.
Śambho	: Epithet of Śiva.
Samudramanthana	: The act of churning of the sea by the gods and demons referred to in Hindu mythology.
Śaṅkara	: Epithet of Śiva, the Destroyer God. The Third deity of the Hindu Trinity, the other two being Brahmā and Viṣṇu.
Sati	: A virtuous woman.
Satyabhāmā	: Daughter of Satrājita and spouse of Kṛṣṇa.
Sītā	: Wife of Śrī Rāma.
Śiva	: Epithet of Śaṅkara.
Śloka	: A stanza.
Somala	: White arsenic.
Stuti	: Praise.
Sudāmā	: The fellow-student of Lord Kṛṣṇa.
Śuka	: Name of a great sage; son of Vyāsa.
Tāṭakā	: Name of a female demon, who was killed by God Rāma.
Trilokisundari	: Universe in the form of a beautiful woman.

Tulasīdāsa : A great Indian poet-saint; author of *Rāmacaritamānasa* in Hindi.

Upamanyu : Name of the lad of a poor brahmin.
Upasaṁhāra : Summing up.
Uśśāpa : A mitigation of curse.

Vaiṣṇava : One of the Hindu sects.
Vālmikī : The author of the great Rāmāyaṇa epic.
Varāha : Boar.
Veda : The oldest and the most revered of the Hindu scriptures. The four Vedas are the Ṛg-Veda, the Yajur-Veda, the Sāma-Veda and the Atharva-Veda.
Vidura : Name of Dhṛtarāṣtra's younger brother (in the Mahābhārata epic).
Viṣṇu : The second deity of the Hindu Trinity who sustains the universe, the other two being Brahmā and Śiva.
Vṛtta : Metre.
Vyāsa : A celebrated sage; author of the Mahābhārata epic and the eighteen Purāṇas.

Yama : The God of death.
Yamunā : A holy river that joins Gaṅgā at Prayāga.

Yaśodā : The foster-mother of Lord Kṛṣṇa who brought him up with great love in his childhood.
Yoga : Religious meditation.

REFERENCE BOOKS

(1) Subodha Kekāvali—Ed. B.A. Bhide

(2) Śloka Kekāvali—Ed. S.N. Banahatti

(3) Moropanta—Life and Literature—Ed. L.R. Pangarkara

(4) Maharashtra-Kavivarya-Moropanta Kṛta, SPHUTA-KAVYE Part-I (Edited with critical and explanatory notes by Vāman Dāji Oka, 1896).

INDEX